Contents

D0534075

Beer and Edam Spread

2 7-ounce rounds Edam cheese

● Bring cheese to room temperature. Cut a circle from the top of each cheese round, about ½ inch from edge. Remove the cut circle of paraffin coating. Carefully scoop cheese out, leaving ½ inch of cheese intact to form a shell. Set shells aside.

1 8-ounce carton dairy sour cream
¼ cup beer
2 teaspoons snipped chives

● Place sour cream, beer, chives, and cheese in a blender container or food processor bowl. Cover and process till smooth, stopping machine occasionally to scrape down sides.

Snipped chives (optional)
Assorted crackers

● Spoon cheese mixture into shells. Cover and chill several hours or overnight. (Cover and chill any remaining cheese mixture and use it to refill shells.) Garnish with chives, if desired. Serve with crackers. Makes 3 cups.

Use a spoon to carefully scoop the cheese out, leaving a ½-inch shell. Break the cheese up into fairly small pieces as you put it into the blender or food processor.

Use a sharp knife to cut a circle through the waxy shell. Cut the scalloped design that's shown with a knife or an apple corer.

Better Homes and Gardens®

Anytime Appetizers

BETTER HOMES AND GARDENS® BOOKS

Editor: Gerald M. Knox
Art Director: Ernest Shelton
Managing Editor: David A. Kirchner
Copy and Production Editors: Marsha Jahns,
    Mary Helen Schiltz, Carl Voss, David A. Walsh

Food and Nutrition Editor: Nancy Byal
Department Head—Cook Books: Sharyl Heiken
Associate Department Heads: Sandra Granseth,
    Rosemary C. Hutchinson, Elizabeth Woolever
Senior Food Editors: Julia Malloy, Marcia Stanley,
    Joyce Trollope
Associate Food Editors: Barbara Atkins, Linda Foley,
    Linda Henry, Lynn Hoppe, Jill Johnson, Mary Jo Plutt,
    Maureen Powers, Martha Schiel
Recipe Development Editor: Marion Viall
Test Kitchen Director: Sharon Stilwell
Test Kitchen Photo Studio Director: Janet Pittman
Test Kitchen Home Economists: Jean Brekke, Kay Cargill,
    Marilyn Cornelius, Jennifer Darling, Maryellyn Krantz,
    Lynelle Munn, Dianna Nolin, Marge Steenson,
    Cynthia Volcko

Associate Art Directors: Linda Ford Vermie, Neoma Alt West,
    Randall Yontz
Assistant Art Directors: Lynda Haupert, Harijs Priekulis,
    Tom Wegner
Senior Graphic Designers: Mike Eagleton, Lyne Neymeyer,
    Stan Sams
Graphic Designers: Mike Burns, Sally Cooper, Darla Whipple-Frain,
    Brian Wignall

Vice President, Editorial Director: Doris Eby
Executive Director, Editorial Services: Duane L. Gregg

Senior Vice President, General Manager: Fred Stines
Director of Publishing: Robert B. Nelson
Vice President, Retail Marketing: Jamie Martin
Vice President, Direct Marketing: Arthur Heydendael

ANYTIME APPETIZERS

Editor: Linda Henry
Copy and Production Editor: Carl Voss
Graphic Designer: Lyne Neymeyer
Electronic Text Processor: Donna Russell
Contributing Photographer: Mike Dieter
Food Stylists: Jill Mead, Janet Pittman
Contributing Illustrator: Thomas Rosborough

On the cover: *Super Nachos*
(see recipe, page 20)

Transfer the cheese
mixture from the blender
or food processor to the
cheese shells. Cover filled
shells (and any extra
spread) with clear plastic
wrap and chill till
serving time.

Salmon Supreme Ball

1 8-ounce package cream
  cheese
1 cup shredded cheddar
  cheese (4 ounces)
1 7¾-ounce can salmon,
  drained, boned, and
  finely flaked
½ teaspoon dried dillweed
¼ cup onion salad dressing

● Bring cream cheese and cheddar cheese to room temperature. In a mixer bowl beat cheeses, salmon, and dillweed with an electric mixer till combined. Gradually add the onion salad dressing, beating till fluffy. Cover and chill for several hours or overnight. (May be stored up to 5 days.)

Save money by buying pink or chum salmon rather than the more expensive red varieties.

Snipped parsley
Assorted crackers

● Before serving, shape salmon mixture into a ball or log, then roll in parsley. Serve with crackers. Makes 1 ball or log (about 2½ cups).

Chutney Cheese Ball

2 cups shredded sharp
  cheddar cheese
  (8 ounces)
2 tablespoons butter *or*
  margarine
⅓ cup milk
1 teaspoon Worcestershire
  sauce
  Dash bottled hot pepper
  sauce
⅓ cup finely chopped
  chutney

● Bring cheese and butter or margarine to room temperature. In a mixer bowl beat with an electric mixer till combined. Add milk, Worcestershire sauce, and hot pepper sauce, beating till combined. Stir in chutney. Cover and chill for several hours or overnight.

Ball, log, circle, heart— shape this peppy cheese mixture to fit your mood or the occasion.

⅓ cup finely chopped pecans
  or peanuts
  Assorted crackers

● Before serving, shape cheese mixture into a ball, then roll in pecans or peanuts. Serve with crackers. Makes 1 ball (about 2 cups).

Cool-as-a-Cucumber Dip

½ cup plain yogurt
½ cup dairy sour cream
¼ teaspoon salt
¼ teaspoon dried dillweed
   Dash bottled hot pepper
    sauce
1 small cucumber, seeded
   and finely chopped
   (about ¾ cup)

● In a medium bowl combine yogurt, sour cream, salt, dillweed, and hot pepper sauce. Pat chopped cucumber dry with paper towels, then stir it into yogurt mixture. Cover and chill several hours or overnight.

For special occasions, create an elegant, European-style appetizer by serving thin slices of smoked salmon on melba toast, topped with a dollop of Cool-as-a-Cucumber Dip.

1 tablespoon chopped green
   onion
1 *or* 2 thin cucumber slices
   Assorted vegetable
    dippers *or* crackers

● Before serving, garnish with onion and cucumber slices. Serve with vegetable dippers or crackers. Makes about 1⅓ cups.

Vegetable Dippers and Dunkers

When a recipe calls for vegetable dippers, don't be satisfied with just carrot and celery sticks—branch out. Include fresh mushrooms, cherry tomatoes, radishes, green pepper strips or rings, zucchini or cucumber spears, and green onions. Or try crisp-cooked baby carrots, kohlrabi sticks, asparagus spears, brussels sprouts, and cauliflower or broccoli flowerets (you can serve them raw if you like).

Arrange the vegetables around a bowl of dip on a bed of lettuce, a tray of crushed ice, or a serving plate. Then let the arrangement double as a table centerpiece.

Taco-Beef Dip

1 **pound lean ground beef** 1 **clove garlic, minced**	● In a 10-inch skillet cook ground beef and garlic till beef is browned. Drain fat.
1 **15-ounce can tomato sauce** ½ **of a 1¼-ounce envelope taco seasoning mix (about 2 tablespoons)** **Several dashes bottled hot pepper sauce**	● Stir in tomato sauce, taco seasoning mix, and hot pepper sauce. Simmer, uncovered, for 5 minutes.
2 **cups shredded cheddar *or* Monterey Jack cheese (8 ounces)** 1 **tablespoon all-purpose flour**	● Toss cheese with flour. Add cheese to meat mixture, a little at a time, stirring just till melted.
Dairy sour cream 1 **small tomato, chopped** 1 **tablespoon sliced green onion** **Tortilla chips, corn chips, *or* Tortilla Crisps (see recipe, page 25)**	● Transfer the hot mixture to a fondue pot or chafing dish, then place over burner. Dollop with sour cream. Garnish with tomato and green onion. Serve with tortilla chips, corn chips, or Tortilla Crisps. Makes 3½ cups.

By using your microwave oven, you'll be eating this spicy dip in next to no time. In a nonmetal casserole dish micro-cook the ground beef and garlic on 100% power (HIGH) for 4 to 5 minutes, stirring once to break up the meat. Drain off the fat. Stir in tomato sauce, taco seasoning mix, and hot pepper sauce. Micro-cook for 3 minutes.

Toss cheese with flour. Gradually stir cheese into meat mixture. Micro-cook for 2 to 3 minutes, stirring every 30 seconds, or till heated through and cheese melts. Serve as directed at left.

Attention Microwave Owners

Microwave recipes were tested in countertop microwave ovens that operate on 600 to 700 watts. Cooking times are approximate since microwave ovens vary by manufacturer. If yours has fewer watts, foods may take a little longer to cook.

Keeping hot dips hot needn't be a problem. Here are some suggestions to help you avoid running back and forth to the kitchen.

Heat and keep food warm in a fondue pot or an electric slow crockery cooker. Or, heat the dips on the stove and transfer them to a ceramic pot or a clay pot—both hold heat a long time. Still another option is to place the serving container on an electric hot tray to keep the dip warm.

P.S. Reheating dips goes faster if you remove them from the refrigerator about 30 minutes before serving.

Layered Cheese and Pesto

Pesto Filling	● Prepare Pesto Filling. Set aside.	**Pesto usually is tossed with hot cooked pasta or vegetables. But we've put it between layers of rich cheeses and cream for this dramatic spread.**
1 **8-ounce package cream cheese** 1 **4½-ounce round Camembert *or* Brie cheese, rind removed** ½ **cup whipping cream**	● Bring cream cheese and Camembert or Brie cheese to room temperature. In a small mixer bowl beat cheeses together with an electric mixer till nearly smooth. In a small mixing bowl beat whipping cream till soft peaks form. Fold whipped cream into cheese mixture.	
	● Line a 3½- to 4-cup mold with plastic wrap. Spread *one-fourth* of the cheese mixture into prepared mold. Spread *one-third* of the Pesto Filling over the cheese mixture. Repeat cheese and pesto layers twice more. Spread remaining cheese mixture on top. Cover and chill for several hours or overnight.	
Paprika (optional) **Fresh basil** **Assorted crackers *or* French bread**	● Before serving, invert mold onto a serving plate. Remove mold and carefully peel off plastic wrap. Sprinkle with paprika, if desired. Garnish with basil. Serve with crackers or thin slices of French bread. Makes 3½ cups.	
	● **Pesto Filling:** In a blender container or food processor bowl combine 1 cup firmly packed snipped *fresh basil;* ¾ cup grated *Parmesan or Romano cheese;* ½ cup firmly packed snipped *parsley;* ¼ cup *pine nuts, walnuts, or almonds;* and 2 cloves *garlic,* quartered. Cover and process with several on/off turns till a paste forms. (Stop machine occasionally to scrape down sides.) With machine running slowly, gradually add ⅓ cup *olive oil or cooking oil* and process to the consistency of soft butter. Makes about 1 cup.	**If fresh basil is hard to come by, use all snipped *parsley* for this pesto (a total of 1½ cups firmly packed). Then add 1 teaspoon dried *basil,* crushed, and continue as directed.**

Shrimp Mousse

1 10¾-ounce can
   condensed cream of
   shrimp soup
½ cup cold water
2 envelopes unflavored
   gelatin
¼ teaspoon pepper

● In a medium saucepan stir together soup, cold water, gelatin, and pepper. Let stand 10 minutes. Cook and stir over low heat till gelatin is dissolved. Remove from heat and cool slightly.

For a large gathering, try serving this Easy Chili-Bean Dip along with the Shrimp Mousse.

Combine one 16-ounce can *refried beans*; one 11-ounce can *condensed cheddar cheese soup*; one 4-ounce can diced *green chili peppers*, drained; and 2 tablespoons *milk*. Heat slowly, stirring frequently, till smooth. Serve warm with corn chips, tortilla chips, crackers, or celery sticks. Makes 3¾ cups.

1 cup cream-style cottage
   cheese
1 cup mayonnaise *or* salad
   dressing
½ cup plain yogurt
1 tablespoon lemon juice
1 6-ounce package frozen
   cooked shrimp, thawed
4 hard-cooked eggs, finely
   chopped
2 tablespoons sliced green
   onion

● Use a rotary beater to beat cottage cheese, mayonnaise or salad dressing, yogurt, and lemon juice into gelatin mixture. Set aside a few whole shrimp for garnish, then finely chop the remaining shrimp. Fold chopped shrimp, hard-cooked eggs, and onion into cottage cheese mixture. Line a 6-cup mold with plastic wrap. Transfer shrimp mixture to mold. Cover and chill till firm.

Finely chopped
   hard-cooked eggs
   (optional)
Snipped fresh dill
   (optional)
Party rye bread *or*
   assorted crackers

● Before serving, invert mousse onto a serving plate. Remove mold and carefully peel off plastic wrap. Garnish with reserved shrimp, hard-cooked eggs, and fresh dill, if desired. Serve with rye bread or crackers. Makes about 5 cups.

Peppy Artichoke Spread

1 14-ounce can artichoke
   hearts, drained
1 6-ounce jar marinated
   artichoke hearts,
   drained

● Place drained artichoke hearts in a blender container or food processor bowl. Cover and process until finely chopped, stopping machine to scrape down sides as necessary.

Skip any last-minute hassle by making this artichoke spread in advance. Freeze the spread in a covered 1-quart container. When ready to serve, let it thaw at room temperature or use your microwave to speed up the defrosting. Place the spread in a 1-quart microwave-safe dish and defrost, uncovered, on 30% power (LOW) for 20 minutes. Heat as directed at left.

1 cup shredded cheddar
   cheese (4 ounces)
1 4-ounce can diced green
   chili peppers, drained
Party rye *or* pumpernickel
   bread

● Transfer artichokes to a medium saucepan, then stir in cheese and chili peppers. Cook and stir over medium-low heat for 12 to 15 minutes or till heated through and cheese is melted. Serve warm with rye or pumpernickel bread. Makes about 2½ cups.

Roast Beef and Radish Spread

1 8-ounce package cream cheese, softened
2 tablespoons mayonnaise *or* salad dressing
2 tablespoons Dijon-style mustard
1 teaspoon prepared horseradish

● In a mixer bowl beat cream cheese, mayonnaise or salad dressing, mustard, and horseradish with an electric mixer till fluffy.

Stir 1 tablespoon *milk* into this spread if it gets a little stiff after chilling.

12 ounces finely chopped cooked beef
½ cup finely chopped radishes
2 green onions, finely chopped
Snipped parsley (optional)
Party rye *or* pumpernickel bread

● Fold in the cooked beef, radishes, and green onion. Cover and chill mixture several hours or overnight. Garnish with parsley, if desired. Serve with rye or pumpernickel bread. Makes about 2½ cups.

Rumaki Spread

6 slices bacon

● In a 10-inch skillet cook bacon till crisp. Drain bacon, reserving 1 tablespoon drippings. Crumble bacon. Set aside.

Japanese rumaki is chicken livers and water chestnuts rolled in bacon strips. We combined the same ingredients differently, to come up with this slightly chunky spread.

8 ounces chicken livers
¼ cup finely chopped onion

● Cook chicken livers and onion in bacon drippings about 5 minutes or till livers are no longer pink, stirring occasionally. Drain liver-onion mixture on paper towels.

2 tablespoons dry sherry
¼ teaspoon salt
⅛ teaspoon garlic powder
Several dashes bottled hot pepper sauce
1 8-ounce can water chestnuts, drained and finely chopped

● Put drained mixture, sherry, salt, garlic powder, and hot pepper sauce into a blender container or food processor bowl. Cover and process till smooth. Stir in water chestnuts and reserved bacon. Line a 1-quart bowl or mold with plastic wrap. Spoon mixture into bowl or mold. Cover and chill for several hours or overnight.

Chopped hard-cooked eggs (optional)
Snipped chives (optional)
Snipped parsley (optional)
Assorted crackers

● Before serving, invert spread onto a serving plate. Remove mold and carefully peel off plastic wrap. Garnish with hard-cooked eggs, chives, or parsley, if desired. Serve with crackers. Makes about 1½ cups.

Seafood Cheese Round

2 8-ounce packages cream
   cheese, softened
¼ cup mayonnaise *or* salad
   dressing
2 tablespoons lemon juice
1 teaspoon Worcestershire
   sauce
   Dash garlic powder
½ cup finely chopped celery
1 tablespoon snipped chives
   (optional)

● In a mixer bowl beat cream cheese, mayonnaise or salad dressing, lemon juice, Worcestershire sauce, and garlic powder with an electric mixer till smooth. Stir in celery and chives, if desired.

Keep this quick and easy recipe in mind for potlucks and parties—it makes a great portable appetizer.

¾ cup chili sauce
2 tablespoons sweet pickle
   relish
1 4½-ounce can small
   shrimp, rinsed and
   drained
1 6-ounce can crab meat,
   drained, flaked, and
   cartilage removed
2 tablespoons snipped
   parsley
   Assorted crackers

● Spread cream cheese mixture into a 9-inch pie plate. Combine chili sauce and pickle relish, then spread it over the cream cheese mixture. Sprinkle shrimp and crab meat over chili sauce mixture. Sprinkle parsley over all. Cover and chill several hours. Serve with crackers. Makes 10 to 12 servings.

Broccoli Dip

2 10-ounce packages frozen
   cut broccoli in cheese
   sauce
⅔ cup dairy sour cream
2 tablespoons lemon juice
2 teaspoons minced dried
   onion

● Prepare broccoli in cheese sauce according to package directions. Place cooked broccoli mixture in a blender container or food processor bowl. Add sour cream, lemon juice, and onion. Cover and process till smooth, stopping machine occasionally to scrape down sides. Transfer dip to a serving bowl. Cover and chill for several hours or overnight.

Want extra flavor? Stir 1 teaspoon dried *thyme*, crushed, into the pureed mixture before chilling.

Milk
Assorted vegetable
   dippers
Breadsticks

● Before serving, stir a little bit of milk into dip, if necessary, to make of dipping consistency. Serve with vegetable dippers and breadsticks. Makes 3 cups.

Green Goddess Dip

½ cup dairy sour cream
½ cup mayonnaise *or* salad dressing
½ cup lightly packed parsley *or* watercress
1 tablespoon anchovy paste
2 teaspoons lemon juice
1 teaspoon dried tarragon, crushed
1 green onion, cut up
1 clove garlic, minced
  Assorted vegetable dippers

● In a blender container or food processor bowl combine sour cream, mayonnaise or salad dressing, parsley or watercress, anchovy paste, lemon juice, dried tarragon, green onion, and garlic. Cover and process till smooth. Cover and chill for several hours or overnight. Serve with assorted vegetable dippers. Makes 1⅓ cups.

The ingredients of the classic, creamy-rich salad dressing are transformed into a delicious dip for raw vegetables—especially fresh mushrooms and cherry tomatoes.

Blue Cheese and Brandy Cheese Ball

2 cups shredded cheddar cheese (8 ounces)
1 8-ounce package cream cheese
½ cup crumbled blue cheese
3 tablespoons brandy
2 tablespoons finely chopped onion
1 tablespoon Worcestershire sauce
  Dash bottled hot pepper sauce
  Dash garlic powder

● Bring cheddar cheese, cream cheese, and blue cheese to room temperature. In a mixer bowl beat cheeses, brandy, onion, Worcestershire sauce, hot pepper sauce, and garlic powder together with an electric mixer till combined. Cover and chill for several hours or overnight.

cheddar cheese

cream cheese

blue cheese

+ brandy
_____
= 1 sensational cheese ball!

¼ cup snipped parsley
¼ cup finely chopped toasted almonds
  Assorted crackers

● Before serving, shape cheese mixture into a ball. Combine parsley and almonds. Roll cheese ball in the parsley-almond mixture. Serve with crackers. Makes 1 ball (about 2⅔ cups).

Oven-Fried Potato Skins

medium baking potatoes (about 3 pounds)

● Scrub potatoes thoroughly and prick with a fork. Bake in a 425° oven about 40 minutes or till done. Halve each potato lengthwise. Scoop out the inside of each potato half, leaving about a ⅜-inch-thick shell. (See photo, below. Reserve cooked potato for another use—see suggestions at right.) Cut *each* potato shell in half lengthwise, making 48 quarters.

If you're wondering what to do with all the leftover cooked potato, why not make a couple of loaves of potato bread, a big pot of potato soup, or some home-style potato patties?

Butter *or* margarine, melted
Grated Parmesan cheese (optional)
Zesty Salsa Cruda *or* Beer-Cheese Sauce (see recipes, page 18)

● Brush potato quarters, inside and out, with melted butter or margarine. Place quarters, cut side up, in a single layer on a large baking sheet. Bake in a 425° oven about 15 minutes or till crisp. Shake cooked quarters in a paper bag with Parmesan cheese, if desired. Top with Zesty Salsa Cruda or Beer-Cheese Sauce. Serve warm. Makes 48.

Cut baked potato in half lengthwise. Using a spoon, scoop out the inside of the potato, leaving about a ⅜-inch-thick shell.

Salsa Cruda

4 medium tomatoes (1½
   pounds), peeled and
   finely chopped
   (about 2 cups)
1 4-ounce can diced green
   chili peppers, drained
¼ cup chopped green onion
¼ cup chopped green pepper
2 tablespoons snipped fresh
   cilantro *or* parsley
2 tablespoons lemon juice
1 clove garlic, minced
½ teaspoon salt
⅛ teaspoon pepper

● In a medium bowl stir together chopped tomatoes, chili peppers, green onion, green pepper, cilantro or parsley, lemon juice, garlic, salt, and pepper. Cover and chill for several hours or overnight, stirring occasionally. Use in Seven-Layer Spread or serve with tacos or tortilla chips. Makes about 3 cups.

Get double-duty from this peppy sauce by using one cup as a layer in the Seven-Layer Spread on page 22. Serve the recipe variation as a chunky, fresh-tasting topper for Oven-Fried Potato Skins on page 17.

● **Zesty Salsa Cruda:** Place *1 cup* Salsa Cruda and ½ cup *tomato sauce* in a blender container or food processor bowl. Cover and process just till pureed. Stir in remaining Salsa Cruda. Cover and chill for several hours or overnight, stirring occasionally. Spoon over Oven-Fried Potato Skins. Makes about 2 cups.

Beer-Cheese Sauce

¾ cup shredded American
   cheese
1 tablespoon all-purpose
   flour
½ teaspoon dry mustard
   Dash paprika

● Bring cheese to room temperature. In a small bowl toss cheese with flour, dry mustard, and paprika.

Besides on potato skins, this lip-smacking sauce is great as a dip with Tortilla Crisps (see recipe, page 25) or purchased tortilla chips.

⅓ cup beer
   Few dashes bottled hot
   pepper sauce
3 tablespoons milk

● In a small saucepan heat beer and hot pepper sauce just till warm. Gradually add cheese mixture, stirring constantly over medium-low heat till cheese is melted and mixture is smooth. Stir in milk and heat through.

Oven-Fried Potato Skins
   (see recipe, page 17)
4 slices bacon,
   crisp-cooked, drained,
   and crumbled

● Spoon cheese mixture over Oven-Fried Potato Skins. Sprinkle with crumbled bacon. Makes about ¾ cup.

Baked Brie with Strawberries

1 1- to 1½-pound unsliced
   round loaf whole grain
   bread
1 1½- to 2-pound round
   Brie cheese with rind, 6
   to 8 inches in diameter
   Fresh strawberries
   Apple slices
   Lemon juice

● Slice ½ inch off the top of the bread and save for another use. Cut loaf as directed at right. If necessary, trim cheese into a circle 2 inches smaller than the diameter of the bread. Insert cheese into bread, then wrap in foil. Bake in a 350° oven about 30 minutes or till heated through. Top with strawberries and apple slices dipped in lemon juice. Slice into wedges to serve. Serves 16 to 20.

To make a bread shell, insert toothpicks in a circle around the top of the cut loaf, 1 inch from the edge. Use a serrated knife to cut down through the loaf around the toothpicks, leaving a base 1 inch thick. Use your fingers to gently remove the center.

Use your microwave oven to make baked Brie without the bread.
  Place one 4½-ounce round Brie cheese, rind removed, in a small nonmetal shallow baking dish. Sprinkle with broken *pecans or walnuts.*
  Micro-cook, uncovered, on 100% power (HIGH) about 30 seconds or till the cheese begins to melt and lose its shape. Serve immediately with fresh fruit or unsalted crackers.

Super Nachos

Pictured on the cover.

½ of a recipe for Tortilla
    Crisps (see recipe, page
    25) *or* 4 cups tortilla
    chips
½ pound bulk Italian
    sausage, chorizo, *or*
    ground beef

● Spread Tortilla Crisps or tortilla chips about one layer deep (overlapping slightly) on an 11- or 12-inch ovenproof platter. Set platter aside. In a skillet cook Italian sausage, chorizo, or ground beef till browned, then drain off fat. Pat with paper towels to remove additional fat.

Throw together a tossed salad, build a plateful of these nifty nachos, and you've made an easy supper for four!

1½ cups shredded cheddar,
    American, *or* mozzarella
    cheese (6 ounces)

● Sprinkle meat evenly over Tortilla Crisps. Sprinkle cheese over meat. Bake in a 350° oven for 5 to 7 minutes or till cheese melts.

1 8-ounce container
    frozen avocado dip,
    thawed
½ cup dairy sour cream
    Sliced ripe olives
    Sliced jalapeño peppers
    Sliced pickled cherry
    peppers

● Spoon avocado dip over meat and cheese, then top with sour cream. Sprinkle with olives, jalapeño peppers, and cherry peppers. Serve warm. Makes 8 servings.

● **Cheese Nachos:** Spread *Tortilla Crisps or tortilla chips* on a platter as directed above. Sprinkle with 1 cup shredded *Monterey Jack cheese* and ½ cup shredded *cheddar or American cheese.* Bake as directed above. Sprinkle with 2 tablespoons canned *green chili peppers,* seeded and chopped, if desired.

Making Wontons

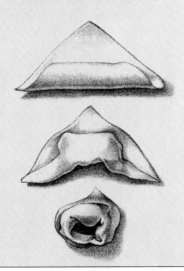

Mastered the egg rolls at right? Use the skins and filling for another Chinese specialty—wontons!

Cut each of the 12 egg roll skins into quarters, making a total of 48 (3½-inch) squares. Position a square with one point toward you. Spoon a scant *1 tablespoon* of the filling just below the center of the square. Fold the bottom point of the square over the filling, tucking the point under the filling.

Roll once toward the center, covering the filling and leaving about 1 inch unrolled at the top of the square. Moisten the right corner of the square with water. Grasp corners and bring them toward you, below the filling, till they meet. Lap the right corner over the left corner, then press to seal securely. Fry wontons in deep hot oil as directed in egg roll recipe.

Egg Rolls

12 egg roll skins
   Chicken-Curry Filling

● Place egg roll skin with one point toward you. Spoon about ¼ cup filling diagonally across and just below center of egg roll skin. Fold bottom point of skin over filling, tucking the point under the filling.

● Fold side corners over, forming an envelope shape. Roll up egg roll toward remaining corner, then moisten point and press firmly to seal. Repeat with the remaining egg roll skins and filling.

Cooking oil for deep-fat frying

● In a heavy saucepan, fry egg rolls, a few at a time, in deep hot oil (365°) for 2 to 3 minutes or till golden brown. Drain on paper towels. Serve warm with one or two sauces (see tip, right). Makes 12 egg rolls.

Half the fun of eating egg rolls and wontons is plunging them into zesty sauces—ones that offer contrasting flavors. For example, match Sweet and Sour Sauce (see recipe, below) with Dijon-style mustard.

Chicken-Curry Filling

2 cups chopped cabbage
2 tablespoons chopped
   green onion
1 clove garlic, minced
1 tablespoon cooking oil
2 cups finely chopped
   cooked chicken

● In a skillet cook cabbage, green onion, and garlic in hot oil for 2 to 3 minutes or till cabbage is crisp-tender. Remove from heat and stir in chicken.

1 beaten egg
2 tablespoons dry red wine
   or water
1 teaspoon curry powder
¼ teaspoon salt

● In a small bowl combine egg, wine or water, curry powder, and salt, then stir into chicken mixture. Use to make Egg Rolls (see recipe, above). Makes 3 cups.

Sweet and Sour Sauce: In a small saucepan combine ½ cup *packed brown sugar* and 1 tablespoon *cornstarch*. Stir in ⅓ cup *chicken broth*, ⅓ cup *red wine vinegar*, 1 tablespoon *soy sauce*, ½ teaspoon *grated gingerroot*, and 2 *cloves garlic*, minced. Cook and stir till thickened and bubbly, then cook and stir for 2 minutes more. Serve warm or cold with Egg Rolls. Makes about 1 cup.

Seven-Layer Spread

1 cup Salsa Cruda (see recipe, page 18)	● Prepare Salsa Cruda several hours ahead or the day before. Thoroughly drain *1 cup* of Salsa Cruda. Set aside.
Picante *or* taco sauce 1 10-ounce can jalapeño bean dip 1 large avocado, seeded, peeled, and cut up 1 tablespoon lemon juice	● In a small bowl add enough picante or taco sauce (about ½ cup) to bean dip to make a spreadable consistency. Set mixture aside. Place avocado and lemon juice in a blender container or food processor bowl. Cover and process till smooth.
Lettuce leaves 1 8-ounce carton dairy sour cream ½ cup shredded Monterey Jack *or* cheddar cheese (2 ounces) 2 tablespoons chopped pitted ripe olives	● Line a large serving platter with lettuce leaves. Spread bean dip mixture over lettuce, making a layer about ¼ inch thick. Spread sour cream evenly over bean dip. Then layer avocado mixture and drained Salsa Cruda. Top with shredded cheese and ripe olives.
Tortilla Crisps (see recipe, page 25) *or* assorted crackers	● Cover and chill for several hours. Serve with Tortilla Crisps or crackers. Makes about 5 cups.

When entertaining your fire-eating friends, increase the hotness level of this colorful spread in a couple of ways: use hot pepper cheese or a jar of the "hot" picante or taco sauce.

But remember—only if you're a hot-food fanatic should you dare do both at the same time!

Beer-Batter Fried Veggies

¾ cup beer ⅔ cup all-purpose flour 1 egg yolk 1½ teaspoons cooking oil	● In a large mixer bowl combine beer, flour, egg yolk, and oil. Beat with an electric mixer on low speed till smooth.
1 egg white	● In a small bowl use a rotary beater to beat egg white till stiff peaks form (tips stand straight). Fold beaten egg white into beer mixture.
4½ to 5 cups fresh whole mushrooms, cauliflower *or* broccoli flowerets, green pepper strips, *or* onion rings Cooking oil for deep-fat frying Buttermilk Dipping Sauce	● Pat vegetables dry with paper towels. Dip vegetables into beer batter. In a heavy saucepan, fry vegetables, a few at a time, in deep hot oil (375°) for 3 to 5 minutes or till golden brown. Drain well. Serve warm with Buttermilk Dipping Sauce. Makes 6 to 8 servings.
	● **Buttermilk Dipping Sauce:** In a small mixing bowl combine ½ cup dairy *sour cream,* ¼ cup *mayonnaise or salad dressing,* 1 tablespoon *milk,* and *half* of a 0.4-ounce envelope *buttermilk salad dressing mix.* Makes ¾ cup sauce.

Keep the cooked veggies warm in a 300° oven while you finish frying the rest.

Deep-Fat Frying Pointers

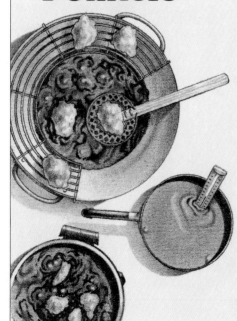

Deep-fried appetizers don't have to be a lot of work if you follow these hints.

● Choose the right pan. An electric deep-fat fryer is one good choice. A wok works well because it has a large cooking surface, as does a heavy skillet or large saucepan that's at least 3 inches deep.

● Use oil that can be heated to a high temperature without smoking. The best bets are corn or peanut oil.

● Use a deep-fat thermometer to keep track of the temperature of the oil while you're frying. Watch the temperature closely. If it's too low, food will be greasy. If it's too high, food will burn before it cooks. (For an accurate reading, the tip of the thermometer shouldn't touch the bottom of the pan.)

● Add food to the hot oil a few pieces at a time. Too much food at once will quickly lower the oil's temperature. And be sure the oil returns to the right temperature between batches.

● When you're all done frying, cool the oil and strain it through cheesecloth. Cover tightly and refrigerate.

Deep-Fried Mozzarella Puffs

10 slices white bread **1½ pounds unsliced mozzarella cheese**	● Remove crusts from bread slices, then cut each slice diagonally into quarters, forming triangles. Cut 40 pieces of cheese the same size and thickness as the bread triangles.	**Other cheeses, such as Swiss, Monterey Jack, or hot pepper cheese, also taste great in these puffs.**
8 eggs **½ cup grated Parmesan cheese**	● In a bowl beat together eggs and Parmesan cheese.	
1 cup all-purpose flour	● To assemble, coat the bread triangles with flour. Then dip each triangle into the beaten egg mixture, allowing excess to drip off. Repeat with cheese triangles. Place one coated cheese triangle on top of each coated bread triangle. (To make ahead, put coated triangles on a baking sheet. Cover with plastic wrap and refrigerate for several hours.)	
Cooking oil for deep-fat frying **½ cup grated Parmesan cheese**	● In a heavy saucepan, fry triangles cheese side down, a few at a time, in deep hot oil (365°) about 2 minutes or till golden brown, turning once. Drain on paper towels. Sprinkle with Parmesan cheese. Serve warm. Makes 40.	

Guacamole with Tortilla Crisps

2 medium avocados **1 medium tomato, peeled and coarsely chopped** **½ of a small onion, cut up** **1 4-ounce can green chili peppers, drained** **1 clove garlic, minced** **1 tablespoon lemon *or* lime juice** **¼ teaspoon salt** **Tortilla Crisps**	● Cut avocados in half lengthwise. Remove seeds and scoop flesh into a blender container or food processor bowl. Add tomato, onion, chili peppers, garlic, lemon or lime juice, and salt. Cover and process till well combined, stopping machine occasionally to scrape down sides. Transfer to a bowl. Cover and chill. Serve with Tortilla Crisps. Makes 2 cups.	**If guacamole (guah-kah-MO-leh) and chips make you thirsty for a pitcher of icy cold Margaritas, see our recipe on page 86.**
	● **Tortilla Crisps:** Cut eight to ten 6-inch *flour tortillas* into wedges. Place in a single layer on an ungreased baking sheet. Bake in a 350° oven about 15 minutes or till dry and crisp.	

Fried Cheese and Broccoli

1 8-ounce package cream cheese	● Bring cream cheese and cheddar cheese to room temperature. In a medium mixer bowl beat cheeses with an electric mixer till combined.
2 cups shredded sharp cheddar cheese (8 ounces)	
1½ cups broccoli *or* cauliflower flowerets	● Mold about *1 tablespoon* cheese mixture around *each* floweret. Cover and chill wrapped flowerets about 1 hour.
1 slightly beaten egg	● For batter, in a medium bowl combine egg, flour, milk, and cooking oil. Beat with a rotary beater just till combined. Carefully dip each chilled broccoli or cauliflower floweret into batter.
1 cup all-purpose flour	
1 cup milk	
2 tablespoons cooking oil	
Cooking oil for deep-fat frying	● In a heavy saucepan fry flowerets, a few at a time, in deep hot oil (365°) for 2 to 3 minutes or till golden brown. Drain on paper towels. Serve warm. Makes about 36 pieces.

Enhance your reputation as a great cook by serving this unique appetizer— fresh vegetables wrapped in cheese, dipped in batter, and deep-fried. Be sure you have plenty!

Fry a few pieces at a time in hot oil. The size of your deep-fat fryer or heavy saucepan will determine the number of pieces you can fry at a time. Drain the cooked vegetables before serving.

Pat flowerets dry with paper towels so cheese mixture will stick. You may need a little more or a little less than 1 tablespoon of cheese, depending on the size of your vegetable pieces.

Just before you're ready to fry the vegetable pieces, dip them into the batter. Let excess batter drip off before you put them into the hot oil.

Snack Mix Ingredients

Tropical

- 1 cup cashews *or* macadamia nuts
- 1 cup coconut chips
- 1 tablespoon soy sauce
- ½ teaspoon garlic powder
- ½ teaspoon ground ginger

Barbecue

- 1 cup peanuts
- 1 tablespoon Worcester- shire sauce
- 1 teaspoon barbecue spice
  Dash garlic powder

Hot and Spicy

- 1 cup peanuts
- 2 teaspoons chili powder
- 1 teaspoon garlic powder
- 1 teaspoon bottled hot pepper sauce

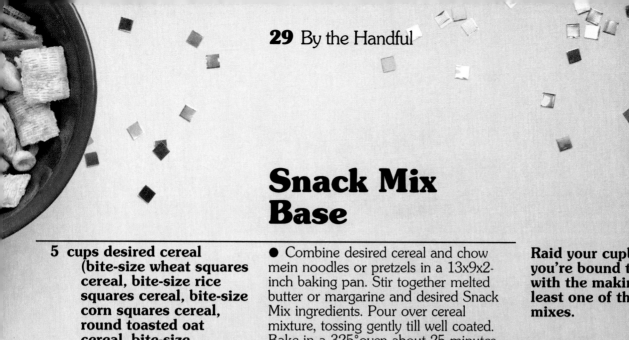

Snack Mix Base

5 cups desired cereal
     (bite-size wheat squares
     cereal, bite-size rice
     squares cereal, bite-size
     corn squares cereal,
     round toasted oat
     cereal, bite-size
     shredded wheat
     biscuits, *or* crispy corn
     and rice cereal bites)
1½ cups chow mein noodles
     or pretzels
⅓ cup butter *or* margarine,
     melted
     Snack Mix Ingredients
     (see choices below)

● Combine desired cereal and chow mein noodles or pretzels in a 13x9x2-inch baking pan. Stir together melted butter or margarine and desired Snack Mix ingredients. Pour over cereal mixture, tossing gently till well coated. Bake in a 325° oven about 25 minutes, stirring once or twice. Spread in a large shallow pan or on foil to cool. Makes about 7½ cups.

Raid your cupboards—you're bound to come up with the makings for at least one of these six mixes.

Herbed Pecan

1 cup broken pecans
1 tablespoon dried parsley
    flakes
1 teaspoon dried thyme,
    crushed
½ teaspoon celery salt
½ teaspoon onion powder

Curry

1 cup peanuts
2 teaspoons curry powder
½ teaspoon crushed red
    pepper
¼ teaspoon onion salt

Traditional

1 cup mixed nuts
1 tablespoon Worcester-
    shire sauce
½ teaspoon seasoned salt
    Dash garlic powder

Five-Spice Walnuts

3 tablespoons butter *or*
  margarine
1 teaspoon five-spice
  powder
½ teaspoon salt
3 cups broken walnuts

● In a medium saucepan melt butter or margarine. Stir in five-spice powder and salt. Add broken walnuts, stirring till nuts are evenly coated.

● Transfer nut mixture to a 13x9x2-inch baking pan. Bake in a 300° oven for 20 minutes, stirring once or twice. Cool in pan for 15 minutes. Turn out onto paper towels to finish cooling. Store tightly covered. Makes 3 cups.

Although you can find five-spice powder in the Oriental section of your grocery store, check your spice rack first. If you have all the spices on hand you can make your own and save yourself a trip to the store. Here's how:

   Combine 1 teaspoon *ground cinnamon;* **1 teaspoon crushed** *aniseed* **or 1** *star anise,* **ground;** ¼ **teaspoon crushed** *fennel seed;* ¼ **teaspoon freshly ground** *pepper* **or** ¼ **teaspoon** *Szechuan pepper;* **and** ⅛ **teaspoon** *ground cloves.* **Store in an airtight container. Makes about 1 tablespoon.**

Glazed Pecans

Butter *or* margarine

● Line a baking sheet with foil. Butter the foil, then set baking sheet aside.

2 cups pecan halves, walnut
  halves, *or* cashews
½ cup sugar
2 tablespoons butter *or*
  margarine

● In a heavy 10-inch skillet combine nuts, sugar, and butter or margarine. Cook and stir over medium heat for 8 to 9 minutes or till sugar melts and turns a rich brown color.

½ teaspoon vanilla

● Remove skillet from heat. Immediately stir in vanilla. Spread nut mixture onto the prepared baking sheet. Cool. Break up mixture into clusters. Store tightly covered. Makes 2 cups.

Close your eyes as you bite into these sugar-coated pecans and imagine you're eating pecan pie.

Caramel Cereal Mix

3 cups bite-size
   shredded wheat biscuits
3 cups round toasted oat
   cereal
2 cups pretzel sticks,
   broken
1½ cups salted peanuts

● Combine shredded wheat biscuits, toasted oat cereal, pretzels, and peanuts in a large buttered roasting pan.

Fill a box or can full of this buttery crunchy mix when you need a special gift and wrap it in brightly colored paper and ribbon. Whoever is lucky enough to get your package will have as much fun eating the mix as you did making it. And don't forget to tuck in a copy of the recipe—it's sure to be in demand.

1⅓ cups sugar
 ¾ cup butter *or* margarine
 ½ cup light corn syrup
 1 teaspoon vanilla

● Butter the sides of 2-quart saucepan. In the pan combine sugar, butter or margarine, and corn syrup. Cook over medium heat to boiling, stirring constantly with a wooden spoon to dissolve sugar. Cook, stirring frequently, till thermometer registers 280°, soft-crack stage. This should take about 10 minutes. Remove saucepan from heat and stir in vanilla.

● Immediately pour syrup mixture over cereal mixture. Stir gently to coat cereal. Bake in a 350° oven about 20 minutes or till golden brown, stirring once.

● Transfer cereal mixture onto a large piece of foil. Cool. Break up cereal mixture into small clusters. Store tightly covered. Makes 12 cups.

Nacho Popcorn

1 teaspoon paprika
½ teaspoon crushed
   red pepper
½ teaspoon ground cumin
¼ cup butter *or* margarine,
   melted
10 cups warm popped
   popcorn
⅓ cup grated Parmesan
   cheese

● In a small bowl stir paprika, red pepper, and cumin into melted butter or margarine. Gently toss butter mixture with popcorn, coating evenly. Sprinkle with Parmesan cheese and toss till coated. Makes 10 cups.

The next time the between-meal munchies hit you, fight back with this spicy popcorn treat.

Got leftover homemade chips, or maybe a bag of stale commercial chips? Use some microwave magic to recrisp them. Spread 1 cup of chips, pretzels, crackers, or other snacks in a shallow nonmetal baking dish. Micro-cook, uncovered, on 100% power (HIGH) for 30 to 45 seconds. Let stand 1 minute and voilà! Fresh snacks!

Homemade Potato Chips

3 medium potatoes	● Scrub potatoes. Use a vegetable peeler to cut *unpeeled* potatoes lengthwise into very thin slices. Pat potato slices dry with paper towels.
Cooking oil for deep-fat frying Salt, onion salt, *or* garlic salt (optional)	● In a heavy saucepan fry potato slices, a few at a time, in deep hot oil (365°) for 1½ minutes or till crisp and golden brown. Drain on paper towels. Sprinkle hot potato slices with salt, onion salt, or garlic salt to taste, if desired. Makes about 7½ cups.

Spicy Cornmeal Crackers

¾ **cup all-purpose flour**
¼ **cup yellow cornmeal**
½ **teaspoon chili powder**
¼ **teaspoon salt**
⅛ **teaspoon garlic powder**
⅛ **teaspoon ground red pepper**
3 **tablespoons milk**
2 **tablespoons cooking oil**

● In a small bowl combine flour, cornmeal, chili powder, salt, garlic powder, and red pepper. Add milk and oil all at once, then stir with a fork till well combined. Form mixture into a ball.

With chili powder, garlic powder, and crushed red pepper, these crackers are mouth-tinglers that will become household favorites.

1 **slightly beaten egg white**

● Place ball between 2 sheets of waxed paper. Roll out into a 12-inch square, then carefully remove waxed paper. Brush square with egg white. Cut into 2-inch squares or diamonds. Transfer to an ungreased baking sheet.

● Bake in a 450° oven about 8 minutes or till lightly browned. Remove from baking sheet immediately. Cool on a wire rack. Store in an airtight container. Makes 36 crackers.

Poppy Seed Crisps

1 **cup whole wheat flour**
½ **teaspoon baking powder**
¼ **teaspoon salt**
⅓ **cup butter** *or* **margarine**
¾ **cup cream-style small-curd cottage cheese**
1 **tablespoon poppy seed**

● In a medium mixing bowl combine flour, baking powder, and salt. Cut in butter or margarine till mixture resembles coarse crumbs. Stir in cottage cheese and poppy seed till mixture forms a ball. Knead gently on a lightly floured surface for 10 to 15 strokes.

Can't be bothered making homemade crackers? They're really as easy as rolled cookies. And you'll be glad you went to the extra effort when guests reach for one after another.

● Divide dough in half. Roll each half into a 16x12-inch rectangle, then cut into 2-inch squares. Prick each square several times with a fork. Place squares on an ungreased baking sheet.

● Bake in a 325° oven about 18 minutes or till golden brown. Remove from baking sheet immediately. Cool on a wire rack. Store in an airtight container. Makes 96 crackers.

Video Vittles

Tune in to easy entertaining when you throw a video party.

Whether you invite friends over to enjoy a rented old-west movie on the VCR or ham it up in front of the video camera, you'll want to supply the gang with snacks to munch on during the screening. When your guests arrive, keep these vittles handy for snacking on all evening long. Turn to pages 36 and 37 for the recipes.

MENU
Herb-Buttered
Pocket Wedges
Three-Layer Spread
Zesty Franks

Zesty Franks

Pictured on pages 34–35.

¼ cup beer
2 teaspoons cornstarch
1½ cups bottled hickory
 smoke-flavored
 barbecue sauce
1 10-ounce jar apple jelly
 Several dashes bottled hot
 pepper sauce

● For sauce, in a small saucepan combine beer and cornstarch, then stir in barbecue sauce, apple jelly, and hot pepper sauce. Cook and stir till thickened and bubbly, then cook and stir for 2 minutes more.

1 16-ounce package
 frankfurters (8 to 10) *or*
 1 pound cocktail
 weiners
1½ cups frozen small
 whole onions

● Bias-slice franks into bite-size pieces. Stir franks or cocktail weiners and frozen onions into sauce. Cook till heated through. Serve warm. Makes 6 servings.

MENU COUNTDOWN
1 Day Ahead:
Prepare Three-Layer Spread and refrigerate.
Several Hours Ahead:
Prepare Herb-Buttered Pocket Wedges.
15 Minutes Ahead:
Prepare Zesty Franks and keep warm.
During Party:
Serve Zesty Franks in a microwave-safe dish and reheat in a microwave oven when necessary. *Or,* keep them warm by serving in a fondue pot or chafing dish.

Herb-Buttered Pocket Wedges

Pictured on pages 34–35.

2 large pita bread rounds *or*
 four 7-inch flour
 tortillas

● Cut each pita round or tortilla into 6 wedges. Gently tear or cut pita wedges in half crosswise to make single layers.

3 tablespoons butter *or*
 margarine, melted
¼ teaspoon Dijon-style
 mustard
2 tablespoons snipped
 parsley
½ teaspoon dried basil,
 crushed
 Dash garlic powder *or*
 onion powder

● In a small bowl combine melted butter or margarine and mustard. Brush one side of pita or tortilla wedges with butter-mustard mixture. Arrange wedges in a single layer on a baking sheet. In a small bowl combine parsley, basil, and garlic or onion powder. Sprinkle over the wedges. Bake in a 350° oven for 10 to 15 minutes or till crisp and golden brown. Serve warm or cold. Makes 6 servings.

● **Parmesan Pocket Wedges:**
Prepare *Herb-Buttered Pocket Wedges* as directed above, *except* substitute ¼ cup grated *Parmesan or Romano cheese* for the parsley mixture.

For a flavor switch, next time around make these crisp and crunchy snacks using whole wheat pita bread.

Three-Layer Spread

Pictured on pages 34–35.

1 envelope unflavored gelatin ⅓ cup water	● Line a 1-quart mold with plastic wrap, then set aside. In a small saucepan soften unflavored gelatin in water for 5 minutes. Cook and stir over medium heat till gelatin dissolves.
1 8-ounce carton dairy sour cream	● For first layer, stir together sour cream and *2 tablespoons* of the gelatin mixture. Spread evenly in the bottom of the prepared mold. Chill about 20 minutes or till almost firm.
2 medium avocados, peeled, seeded, and mashed 2 tablespoons mayonnaise *or* salad dressing 2 tablespoons lemon juice ¼ teaspoon salt Dash bottled hot pepper sauce	● Meanwhile, for second layer combine avocados, mayonnaise or salad dressing, lemon juice, salt, hot pepper sauce, and *2 tablespoons* of the gelatin mixture. Spread avocado mixture evenly over the sour cream layer. Chill about 20 minutes or till almost set.
6 hard-cooked eggs, finely chopped ¼ cup mayonnaise *or* salad dressing 2 tablespoons snipped parsley 1 tablespoon chopped green onion ¼ teaspoon salt	● For third layer, combine hard-cooked eggs, mayonnaise or salad dressing, parsley, green onion, salt, and remaining gelatin mixture. Spread evenly over avocado layer. Cover and chill overnight.
1 tablespoon chopped pimiento 1 tablespoon bias-sliced green onion Assorted crackers	● Before serving, invert spread onto a serving platter. Remove mold and carefully peel off plastic wrap. Sprinkle chopped pimiento and sliced green onion over the top. Serve with crackers. Makes 6 to 10 servings.

Mold this party spread in a 1-quart bowl if nothing else is available. Line the bowl with plastic wrap and the spread will release easily.

Wine and Cheese Party— Cheese Sampler

Next time you're planning a get-together—make it a wine-and-cheese-tasting party! It's a fun and easy way for you and your guests to get acquainted with a variety of wines and cheeses. The information on this and the next five pages will help you decide what wines and cheeses to serve together.

To serve the cheese, plan about ¼ pound of cheese per person. Remove the cheeses from the refrigerator about an hour before serving so they will be at their flavor-peak. Set out unsalted crackers and fresh fruit for guests to nibble on between tastings.

Choose as many cheeses as you like from these two pages (also see photo, pages 40–41), being sure to include a balance of strong and mild cheeses as well as textures ranging from soft to hard.

Asiago (ah-see-AH-goh) is a hard cheese with a strong, sharp, and slightly salty flavor. It may or may not be coated with paraffin. Thinly sliced, the cheese is good for sandwiches or snacks, but also can be grated and used like grated Parmesan cheese.

Bel Paese (bel-pah-AY-say) is the consistency of firm butter. It has a slightly gray surface and a creamy yellow interior. The flavor ranges from delicately rich, sweet, and creamy to robust. Serve it with fruit and crackers, or use it like mozzarella in sauces or casseroles.

Blue cheese is the name used for several varieties of blue-veined cheeses. Even though they are all called blue-veined, some cheeses actually can have blue, blue-black, or green veins. Blue cheese is strong and pungent in flavor. Use it in salads and salad dressings or with fruit.

Boursin (boor-SOHN) is a rich, creamy, tangy cheese that is flavored with pepper, garlic, or herbs. In its natural state, boursin is pure white, but when flavorings are added, its color depends upon the flavoring. Serve boursin as an appetizer.

Brick cheese has a mild, sweetish tasting flavor, but at the same time, it has a certain pungency, tanginess, and distinctive aroma. Brick cheese can be aged for up to three months. The younger the cheese, the milder the flavor and the creamier the texture. Serve brick cheese as an appetizer or in sandwiches.

Brie (bree) cheese has a creamy, rich flavor that is both subtle and tangy at the same time. The thin, edible crust is a powdery white, while the interior color varies from cream to golden. Serve Brie with fruit or as an appetizer.

Bruder Basil (BREW-der BAZ-el) is a German cheese with a slightly smoky flavor. It's traditionally served around the holidays as an appetizer.

Camembert (KAM-ehm-berh) is slightly bitter and yeasty in flavor. When the cheese is cut, the soft, almost-fluid consistency of the cheese causes it to bulge out from under its white to off-white edible crust. Serve Camembert as an appetizer or as a dessert with fruit.

Cheddar cheese is naturally white, but usually is colored deep golden-yellow. It frequently is labeled as being mild, medium, or sharp in flavor, with the longer-aged cheddars sharper and more full-bodied. Cheddar is an all-purpose cheese that can be used in salads, sandwiches, sauces, main dishes, or with fruits.

Cheshire (CHEHSH-er) cheese is a crumbly, white- to orange-colored cheese with a musty aroma. The flavor is tangy yet mild. Serve it as an appetizer, a snack, or in sandwiches.

Colby cheese has a texture similar to cheddar cheese, but slightly more granular. The flavor is slightly sweeter than cheddar, but grows stronger with age. This golden-yellow cheese can be used as a snack, or in sandwiches, sauces, or casseroles.

Edam (EE-dam) is a firm-textured cheese shaped into a flattened ball and coated with red paraffin. It has a mild and nutty flavor that works well in appetizers, desserts, or main dishes.

Farmer cheese varies widely in both texture and flavor. Depending on the age of the cheese, it may be dry and crumbly with a slight bitterness or tang, while others are creamy with a very mild flavor. Serve it in salads or with fruit.

Feta (FEHT-ah) is a traditional, soft, white, Greek cheese with a sharp, salty flavor. Its crumbly texture appears wet but feels dry. If you find its flavor to be too sharp or salty, soak it in milk. Serve feta in salads, sandwiches, or casseroles.

Fontina (fon-TEE-nah) has a delicate nutty flavor and a pleasant aroma. This wheel-shaped cheese may have small holes scattered over its smooth, shiny surface. Serve fontina as an appetizer, snack, dessert, or in fondues or casseroles.

Gjetost (YET-ohst), a Norwegian goat cheese, has a distinctive rich brown color and a hard, solid texture. Its color and sweet caramelized flavor are unlike any other cheese. Serve thinly sliced gjetost with fruit or on breads.

Gorgonzola (gor-gon-ZOH-lah), an off-white cheese with greenish-blue veins, has a strong, pungent flavor and aroma. It is creamy and salty, but less salty than blue cheese. Use it as you would other blue cheeses.

Gouda (GOO-dah) has a yellow-orange interior and is coated with a yellow or red wax. It is shaped like a flattened ball. The flavor is mild and slightly nutty, and its texture is smooth and waxy. Serve it as an appetizer, snack, or dessert, or in salads and sandwiches.

Gruyère (groo-YEHR) has a mild, nutlike flavor with a slightly sweetish aftertaste. It is firm-bodied and has small holes or "eyes." Serve Gruyère with fruit or in appetizers, soups, and fondues.

Havarti (ha-VART-ee) is a cream-colored cheese that varies in flavor. Young havarti (aged two to three months) has a mild flavor. When aged longer, havarti acquires a pungent flavor. It has a porous yellow-to-white texture with small, irregular holes. Serve it as an appetizer or snack, in sandwiches, or as a dessert with fruit.

Jarlsberg (YARLS-berg), with its smooth, firm, texture and small holes, looks similar to Swiss, but has a very mild flavor. The cheese has a thick natural rind covered with a yellow wax. The interior is white to light yellow in color. Serve Jarlsberg with fruit or in sandwiches, sauces, or casseroles.

Limburger cheese is famous for its very pungent aroma and flavor; enjoying it is an acquired taste. It has a pale yellow color and a soft, creamy texture. Serve it as a snack or with strong-flavored vegetables, such as onions, radishes, or shallots.

Montery Jack (MONT-er-ay JAK) cheese has a rather chewy consistency. This creamy-white colored cheese has a mild and nutty flavor. Well known for its use in Mexican cooking, you can also serve it as a snack.

Mozzarella cheese has a mild flavor that is creamy and vaguely sweet. The texture is smooth and firm. Because of its mild flavor and creamy consistency, you can use it in almost all types of cooking.

Muenster (MUHN-ster) cheese varies in texture from moist, porous, and spongy to crumbly and dry. Its flavor varies from mild to pungent. Muenster cheese made in the United States or Denmark is usually the mild and moist variety, and that made in Germany is the drier, crumbly, pungent type. Muenster usually is made in wheels and has a thin outer rind. It can be served as a dessert or snack or in sandwiches.

Parmesan is a straw-yellow cheese that tastes slightly nutty and salty. It is a very dry cheese that is made in large wheels. However, the grated form is the most familiar. Parmesan cheese will stay fresh many months because of its low moisture content. Serve it to complement salads, breads, or main dishes.

Port du Salut (pohr-doo-sah-LOO) cheese at first tastes mild, buttery, creamy, and smooth, but later develops a subtle, sharp aftertaste. It is made in small wheels and has a creamy-yellow interior that is covered by a thin orange rind. Serve it as a snack or dessert.

Provolone (proh-voh-LOH-nee) cheese varies from mild to sharp, and has a lightly smoked flavor. It has a light, golden, interior and a brown surface. The texture is firm, compact, and flaky. Use it in appetizers, sandwiches, or snacks.

Romano cheese is a dry, hard cheese that is similar to Parmesan cheese, but has a stronger flavor and aroma. Romano can be used in salads or sandwiches, as a snack, or in pasta dishes. It is usually grated or shredded like Parmesan cheese.

Roquefort (ROHK-fort) cheese is creamy-white in color, with many blue veins. It has a strong, pungent, salty flavor with a lingering aftertaste. Use it as you would other blue cheeses.

Sage Derby is a variation of Derby cheese. Fresh sage leaves have been added to it, giving it a greenish hue. The sage also adds a sharp, fragrant flavor to the cheese. Use Sage Derby in salad dressings, as an appetizer, or crumble it and sprinkle in soups or salads.

Sapsago (sap-SAY-goh) is an unusual cone-shaped cheese with a hard dry texture and a "grassy" flavor. The light green color comes from the large quantity of dried clover added to the curd. Sapsago is a hard grating cheese that can be used in salads or egg dishes.

Stilton often is referred to as the "king" of the blue-veined cheeses. It has a dense but crumbly texture. The flavor is piquant but rich. It is less salty and milder than Roquefort and is less creamy than Gorgonzola. It has a brown-gray rind that is crusty and slightly wrinkled. Serve Stilton with fruit for dessert or use it in salads.

Swiss is a popular cheese with a firm, smooth texture. There are large holes or "eyes" scattered throughout the cheese. It varies in color from off-white to a rich yellow. The sweet and nutty taste makes Swiss excellent as an appetizer or snack or as an ingredient in casseroles, sandwiches, or salads.

1. Cheddar 2. Stilton 3. Sage Derby 4. Port du Salut
5. Vermont White Cheddar 6. Edam 7. Bel Paese
8. Jarlsberg 9. String Mozzarella 10. Blue Cheese
11. Cheshire with Stilton 12. Provolone 13. Gjetost
14. Bruder Basil 15. Sapsago

Wine and Cheese Party— Wine Sampler

Tailor your wine and cheese party to the types of wines that interest you. For a "first-course" tasting, feature appetizer wines such as sherry and vermouth. A "dessert" tasting can focus on sweet dessert wines such as port or cream sherry. Or, if you like, offer a more varied selection of wines that includes reds, whites, and rosés. Plan on serving 1 ounce of each appetizer or dessert wine per person, and 1 to 2 ounces per person of the others. Suggestions for cheeses to accompany the various wines can be found below.

Burgundy
(BUR-gun-dy)
Technically, Burgundy comes from a legally delimited area in France and includes both red and white wines. Because French law reserves the name "Burgundy" only for certain wines, all French Burgundys are better-than-average wines.

Worldwide, the name burgundy is used to describe any full-bodied red wine. If you're looking for an honorable U.S. counterpart of a true French Burgundy, look for bottles labeled Pinot Noir and Gamay-Beaujolais (red), or Chardonnay (white).

Serve with cheddar, Port du Salut, provolone, or Gorgonzola cheeses.

Beaujolais
(BO-zho-lay)
Beaujolais, made from the Gamay grape, is one of the best-loved red wines from the Lyons region of France. It has a fruity, full-bodied, almost spicy flavor, with no trace of harshness.

Each November, another Beaujolais, *Beaujolais Primeur* (also known as *Nouveau*), is made available. The French call it the "wine of the new year." It is a light, almost fizzing, pale red wine that should be used before New Year's Day. Serve both types of Beaujolais with cheddar cheese.

Cabernet Sauvignon
(kab-er-NAY SO-veen-yon)
This great red wine grape, originally from the Bordeaux region of France, is responsible for the high quality of some of the world's most celebrated wines. In France it becomes some of the classic Clarets of Bordeaux. In American wines, the name Cabernet or Cabernet Sauvignon on a wine label is an indication of a superior red wine.

Try serving Cabernet Sauvignon with Brie, Camembert, sharp cheddar, or blue cheeses.

Champagne
Strictly speaking, Champagne means French Champagne: a wine made from only certain varieties of grapes, in a legally delimited region of France.

Other countries have adopted other names for their own sparkling wines, as *sekt* in Germany and *spumante* in Italy. However, in the U.S., any sparkling wine may be called champagne provided it's made by the same bottle-fermented process as French Champagne, and its geographic origin is on the label.

According to the degree of dryness of the wine, champagne may be labeled as follows:
Brut: the driest and least sweet
Extra-Dry: not as dry as brut
Sec: slightly sweet
Demi-Sec: quite sweet

Serve champagnes with Brie or cream cheeses.

Chablis
(shab-LEE)
In France, Chablis is a white wine from the Burgundy region. It has an intensely dry, almost harsh flavor. Its color is a light yellow, with a slightly greenish overtone.

In the U.S., any white table wine can be called "chablis." To find a California counterpart for the fine French wine, look for bottles labeled Chardonnay or Pinot Chardonnay. Serve any chablis with Edam, Gouda, or brick cheeses.

Chenin Blanc
(SHEN-in BLAWN)
This grape is used to make such French white wines as Vouvray and Anjou Blanc. The wines are soft, slightly dry, and nicely fruity.

In the U.S., this varietal wine is sometimes a little sweet with a pleasing perfumed aroma. Serve with Gouda, Edam, or Swiss cheeses.

Chianti
(key-AHN-tee)
Chianti is a red Italian table wine that's famous worldwide, thanks to its straw-covered bottle (fiasco). Within the Chianti region of Italy is a strictly delimited zone where wines may be labeled *Chianti Classico*. Only a *Chianti Classico* carries a seal which consists of a black target with a rooster in the center and varying colors of borders (the border's color indicates the number of years of aging).

California chianti—with or without the fancy bottle—is a blend of red wines. It is ruby red, medium tart, and medium-bodied. Serve chianti with blue cheeses.

French Colombard
Colombard is a productive, good-quality white wine grape, grown principally in the Cognac district of France. In France, it gives an agreeable, though not very distinguished, dry white wine.

In California, this wine is green-gold in color, and has a light, delicate flavor with just enough acid to stimulate the taste buds. Serve with Gouda, Swiss, or Muenster cheeses.

Gewürztraminer
(geb-vert-tra-MEAN-er or geb-woors-tra-mean-AIR)
This tough-skinned, pinkish-blue grape, well known in Germany and the Alsace region of France, makes a distinctive white wine. Spicy and aromatic—there's no mistaking this wine. It's the one you'll remember as "perfumy," and for some people it takes a while to appreciate. The same qualities, though somewhat muted, are found in the American-grown grape. Serve with boursin, Edam, Monterey Jack, Gouda, or Muenster cheeses.

Pinot Noir
(pea-no NWAR)
The Pinot Noir grape is responsible for all fine red French Burgundys. On a California label, Pinot usually assures an above-average wine. A good Pinot Noir is smooth, soft, and light in character. Serve with Gorgonzola, Stilton, or blue cheeses.

Port
Port is a rich, full-bodied wine made in red, white, and amber colors. To make port, fermentation of the original wine is halted with brandy. Ports aged in wooden casks for two or more years are labeled as *ruby* or *tawny*. Tawny is older, browner, less fruity, and usually more expensive than ruby port. *Vintage* port is aged in bottles for at least 10 years after it's been aged in casks for two years.

Serve ruby or tawny port with Edam, Gouda, cream cheese, cheddar, or Camembert cheeses.

Riesling
(REES-ling)
The Riesling grape, from Germany's Rhine and Mosel valleys, is one of the greatest of white wine grapes. The German wine is slightly sweet to very sweet.

In the U.S., wines from the classic German Riesling grape are labeled Johannisberg Riesling or White Riesling. They have a floral aroma, a clean fruity taste, and a good balance of acidity along with a slight sweetness. Other U.S. wines may be labeled riesling if they contain a *variety* of the Riesling grape, such as Grey Riesling or Emerald Riesling. Serve with Muenster, Gouda, or Gruyère cheeses.

Rosé Wines
(ro-ZAY)
Rosé wines are simply pale red wines. The grape skins are removed early in fermentation, before all the usual red color can develop in the wine. Rosés may be sweet or dry or even lightly carbonated. Rosés are produced in almost all wine-growing countries.

There are as many tastes as there are grapes and blends of rosé. The finest rosés are dry, fruity, and fresh tasting. Rosé wines are most flavorful, with their loveliest color, within two years of vintage—so don't try to age them. Serve with mild cheeses such as brick, mozzarella, Muenster, or Jarlsberg.

Sauvignon Blanc
(SO-vee-nyawn BLAWN)
One of the white wine grapes from the Bordeaux region of France, the Sauvignon Blanc grape is used to make the dry wines of Sancerre and Pouilly-Fumé. In the U.S., both dry and sweet Sauvignon Blancs are produced. Some of the dry ones are labeled Fumé Blanc or Blanc Fumé.

Sauvignon Blanc is aromatic, a little spicy, and very fruity. Serve with farmer cheeses or with Swiss or Gruyère cheeses.

Sherry
Sherry is made in many countries of the world, but true sherry comes from Spain. It is a fortified wine, which means that brandy is added before bottling to bring the alcohol content to about 20 percent.

Sherry comes dry or sweet, with many gradations between:
Fino: light and dry; usually served before dinner
Amontillado: medium dry
Manzanilla: very pale and dry
Oloroso: dark and medium-sweet
Cream: sweetened Oloroso

Dry sherries pair nicely with blue cheeses and also with sharp and extra-sharp cheddars. Serve cream sherries with Camembert, Edam, Gouda, or Muenster cheeses.

Vermouth
(ver-MOOTH)
Vermouth is used today principally as an aperitif and as a cocktail ingredient. It's made by adding brandy to wine, then flavoring it with a mixture of up to 50 herbs. Each vermouth manufacturer has his own special recipe.

There are two kinds of vermouth: dry and sweet. Dry vermouth is highly perfumed with herbs and spices and is added sparingly to martini cocktails. Sweet vermouth also has flavorings added, but is mellower and more robust. It is used in manhattan cocktails. Serve dry vermouth with Brie or mild cheddar cheeses.

Zinfandel
(ZIN-fan-dell)
Although it may have Italian origin, Zinfandel is a long-time California specialty grape that's now gaining recognition and popularity. These red wine grapes produce a distinctive wine that may be enjoyed as either a young or aged table wine—or even as a rich, late-harvest wine.

When young, Zinfandel tastes fruity and dry, with a berrylike aroma and flavor. If aged, the bouquet suggests black currants, pepper, herbs, and spice. Serve with Monterey Jack, Edam, Port du Salut, or Bel Paese cheeses.

Glacéed Sandwiches

12	slices rye bread
½	cup dairy sour cream
½	cup chopped nuts
¼	cup creamy Italian salad dressing
½	teaspoon dry mustard
1½	cups shredded cheddar cheese (6 ounces)
12	ounces very thinly sliced fully cooked ham

● Cut each bread slice into a 3- to 4-inch circle or square, removing the crusts. Set bread aside. In a medium bowl combine sour cream, nuts, Italian salad dressing, and mustard. Stir in cheddar cheese. Spread cheese mixture on one side of each piece of bread. Cut 2 or 3 slices of ham to fit each piece of bread. Place atop cheese mixture. Cover sandwiches and chill.

2	teaspoons unflavored gelatin
3	tablespoons cold water
2	cups mayonnaise *or* salad dressing
⅓	cup whipping cream

● In a small saucepan soften gelatin in cold water. Let stand 5 minutes. Cook and stir over low heat till gelatin is dissolved. Remove from heat and cool slightly. In a bowl stir together mayonnaise or salad dressing and whipping cream. Stir in dissolved gelatin.

Assorted toppers (see tip, far right)

● Place chilled sandwiches on a wire rack. Spoon mayonnaise mixture over each sandwich, allowing mixture to drip down the sides of bread to coat evenly. Decorate sandwiches with desired toppers. Cover and chill about 1 hour or till set. Makes 12 sandwiches.

These fancy open-face sandwiches are pretty enough for an appetizer tea and hearty enough for a late-night refreshment.

Use a cookie or hors d'oeuvres cutter to make sandwiches in different shapes.

Spoon the glazing mixture over the open-face sandwiches. Let excess glaze drip down the sides and run off.

Garnish sandwiches with decoratively cut foods to suit your fancy. You might try walnut halves, sliced olives, ham pieces, parsley or watercress, avocado slices, cooked asparagus tips, grapes, or green pepper strips.

Sausage Pâté

¾ **pound bulk pork sausage** ½ **cup chopped onion** 2 **cloves garlic, minced** 4 **ounces chicken livers**	● In a 10-inch skillet cook sausage, onion, and garlic till meat is browned. Add chicken livers to skillet. Cook and stir over high heat about 3 minutes or till liver is no longer pink. Drain well. Cool.
½ **cup dry white wine** ¼ **cup milk** 2 **eggs** 2 **tablespoons fine dry bread crumbs** 1 **tablespoon cornstarch** ¼ **teaspoon salt**	● In a blender container or food processor bowl combine the sausage-liver mixture, wine, and milk. Cover and process till smooth. Add eggs, bread crumbs, cornstarch, salt, and ¼ teaspoon *pepper*. Cover and process thoroughly.
Softened cream cheese (optional) **Assorted crackers**	● Transfer mixture to a greased 7½x3½x2-inch loaf pan. Cover with foil. Place in a shallow baking pan. Pour hot water around loaf pan to a depth of ½ inch. Bake in a 325° oven for 1 hour. Cool thoroughly. Cover and chill for several hours or overnight. Before serving, invert pâté onto a serving plate. Garnish by piping cream cheese around the top, if desired. Serve with crackers. Makes 12 servings.

A trick from our Test Kitchen: Line the loaf pan with greased foil before baking your pâté. Then when you're ready to unmold it, just grab the foil and lift.

Seafood-Cucumber Pâté

1 **envelope unflavored gelatin** ½ **cup cold water**	● In a small saucepan soften gelatin in water. Let stand 5 minutes. Cook and stir over low heat till gelatin is dissolved.
1 **3-ounce package cream cheese, softened** ⅓ **cup buttermilk salad dressing** 2 **tablespoons vinegar** 1 **medium cucumber, seeded and coarsely chopped (about 1½ cups)**	● For cucumber layer, in small mixer bowl beat together cream cheese, salad dressing, and vinegar with an electric mixer. Stir in the cucumber and *half* of the dissolved gelatin. Line an 8x4x2-inch loaf pan with plastic wrap. Transfer mixture to loaf pan. Chill till almost firm (about 45 minutes to 1 hour).
2 **3-ounce packages cream cheese, softened** 1 **7¾-ounce can red salmon, drained, flaked, and skin and bones removed** 1 **4½-ounce can shrimp, rinsed and drained** ⅓ **cup mayonnaise *or* salad dressing** 1 **tablespoon cocktail sauce** **Lettuce leaves** **Assorted crackers**	● For seafood layer, in a medium mixing bowl combine cream cheese, salmon, shrimp, mayonnaise or salad dressing, and cocktail sauce. Stir in remaining dissolved gelatin. Spread over cucumber layer. Chill till set (about 6 hours or overnight). Before serving, invert pâté onto a lettuce-lined platter. Remove pan and carefully peel off plastic wrap. Serve with crackers. Makes 12 servings.

With its pink and green layers, this fresh-tasting spread is perfect for Christmas parties.

Shells of Crab

⅓ cup mayonnaise *or* salad
    dressing
⅓ cup finely chopped onion
1 teaspoon snipped chives
¼ teaspoon dried dillweed
¼ teaspoon Worcestershire
    sauce
½ of a 6-ounce package
    frozen crab meat,
    cooked, drained, and
    flaked (⅔ cup)

● For crab filling, in a small mixing bowl combine mayonnaise or salad dressing, onion, chives, dillweed, and Worcestershire sauce. Stir in crab meat. Chill the filling.

Normally seashell-shape madeleine pans are used to make little French tea cakes. But we dreamed up another use for them— this elegant chive and crab appetizer.

2 cups all-purpose flour
½ teaspoon salt
½ cup shortening
5 to 7 tablespoons cold
    water

● For pastry, in a mixing bowl stir together flour and salt. Cut in shortening till pieces are the size of small peas. Sprinkle *1 tablespoon* of the water over part of the mixture, then gently toss with a fork. Push to side of bowl. Repeat till all is moistened. Form dough into a ball, then divide in half. On a lightly floured surface, flatten each half with your hands, then roll into a 16x8-inch rectangle.

Water

● Place *one* of the rectangles over a madeleine pan. Press pastry into shells. Fill *each* shell with about *1 tablespoon* of crab filling. Brush water around outlines of shells. Place the remaining pastry rectangle over the filled madeleine pan. Press and seal around shells. With a fluted pastry wheel trim around edge of pan, then cut between the shells.

1 slightly beaten egg yolk
1 tablespoon water

● Bake in a 450° oven for 15 minutes. Meanwhile, combine egg yolk and water. Remove partially cooked shells from madeleine pan and invert onto a baking sheet. Brush with egg yolk mixture. Bake for 8 to 10 minutes more or till golden brown. Serve warm. Makes 12.

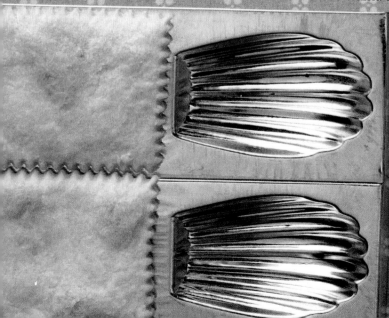

Baby Brie in Phyllo

1 tablespoon apricot preserves 1 4½-ounce round Brie **or** Camembert cheese 3 sheets frozen phyllo dough (18x14-inch rectangles), thawed and halved crosswise 2 tablespoons butter **or** margarine, melted	● Spread preserves on top of Brie or Camembert round. Brush *1 sheet* of the phyllo dough with melted butter or margarine. (Cover the remaining phyllo with a damp cloth to prevent drying.) Wrap phyllo around Brie or Camembert. Turn cheese over. Repeat brushing and wrapping 5 more times. (Turn cheese over after wrapping each sheet for even distribution.) Brush phyllo-wrapped cheese with butter. Cover and chill.
Apple **or** pear slices	● Before serving, place the phyllo-wrapped cheese in a shallow baking pan. Bake in a 425° oven for 8 to 12 minutes or till golden. Let stand for 10 minutes. Serve warm with apple or pear slices. Makes 4 to 6 servings.

Here's how to adapt Baby Brie in Phyllo for a crowd of 24 to 30. Prepare the recipe as directed at left, *except* use: ¼ cup *apricot preserves,* one 2-pound round of *Brie or Camembert cheese,* 12 sheets *phyllo dough,* (18x14-inch rectangles), and ½ cup *butter or margarine.*

Ham and Kraut Balls

½ cup finely chopped onion 1 clove garlic, minced 1 tablespoon butter **or** margarine 3 tablespoons all-purpose flour ½ cup dry white wine **or** water	● In a saucepan cook onion and garlic in butter or margarine till tender but not brown, then stir in flour. Add wine or water all at once. Cook and stir till thickened and bubbly, then cook and stir for 1 minute more. Remove from heat.
1 16-ounce can sauerkraut, rinsed, drained, and very finely chopped 1 6¾-ounce can chunk-style ham, drained and flaked 2 tablespoons snipped parsley ½ teaspoon caraway seed	● Stir sauerkraut, ham, parsley, and caraway seed into onion mixture. Cover and chill at least 1 hour. Form chilled sauerkraut mixture into 1½-inch balls.
⅔ cup all-purpose flour ½ cup milk 1 beaten egg	● For batter, in a bowl beat together flour, milk, and egg until smooth.
1 cup fine dry bread crumbs Cooking oil for deep-fat frying Easy Mustard Sauce (see recipe, right)	● Dip sauerkraut balls in batter, then roll in bread crumbs. In a heavy saucepan, fry sauerkraut balls, a few at a time, in deep hot oil (365°) for 1 minute or till golden brown. Drain well on paper towels. Serve warm with Easy Mustard Sauce. Makes about 24 balls.

This no-cook mustard sauce not only peps up Ham and Kraut Balls, but egg rolls and wontons too.

Easy Mustard Sauce: In a small bowl combine one 8-ounce carton *dairy sour cream,* 2 tablespoons *milk,* and 1 tablespoon *Dijon-style mustard.*

Salmon Phyllo Triangles

2 beaten eggs
1 cup cream-style cottage cheese, drained
½ cup finely chopped cucumber
½ teaspoon dried dillweed
¼ teaspoon lemon pepper
1 7¾-ounce can salmon, drained, boned, and finely flaked

● For filling, in a medium bowl combine eggs, cottage cheese, cucumber, dillweed, and lemon pepper. Gently fold in salmon. Set filling aside.

Add just the right touch of glamour to your next party with these elegant pastry triangles and this party lighting tip: Arrange 7 to 10 large, fat candles on a flat-bottom platter. Place several platters of candles around your house to add soft lighting.

12 sheets phyllo dough (8 to 10 ounces)
¾ cup butter *or* margarine, melted

● Lightly brush *1 sheet* of the phyllo dough with *some* of the melted butter or margarine. Place another sheet of phyllo dough on top of the first sheet, then brush with butter or margarine. Repeat with butter and third sheet of phyllo dough. (Cover the remaining phyllo with a damp cloth to prevent drying.) Cut the stack of 3 buttered sheets lengthwise into 2-inch-wide strips. For each triangle, spoon *1 scant tablespoon* of the salmon filling about 1 inch from one end of *each* strip. Fold the end over the filling at 45-degree angle. Continue folding to form a triangle that encloses the filling, using the entire strip. (See illustration, below.) Repeat 3 more times with the remaining sheets of phyllo dough, butter or margarine, and salmon filling.

● Place triangles on a baking sheet, then brush with butter or margarine. Bake in a 375° oven for 18 to 20 minutes. Serve warm or cool. Makes 32.

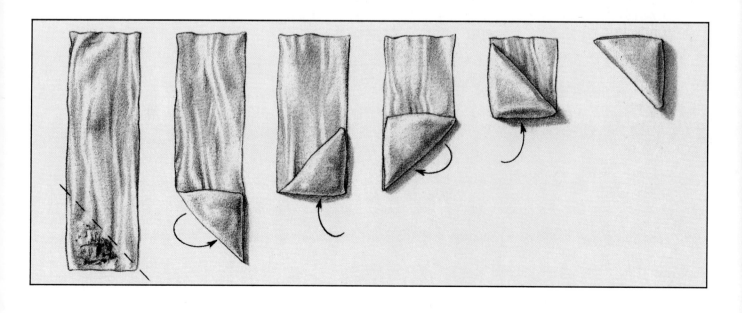

Bite-Size Crab Quiches

1 package (6) refrigerated flaky dinner rolls 1 6-ounce can crab meat, drained, flaked, and cartilage removed ½ cup shredded Swiss cheese (2 ounces)	● Separate each dinner roll into 4 layers. Place *each* section in a greased 1¾-inch-diameter muffin cup, pressing the dough onto bottom and up sides of muffin cup. Sprinkle *1 rounded teaspoon* crab into *each* muffin cup. Sprinkle *1 teaspoon* cheese over crab.
1 egg ½ cup milk ½ teaspoon dried dillweed	● In a bowl combine egg, milk, and dillweed. Spoon about *1½ teaspoons* egg mixture into *each* muffin cup.
	● Bake in a 375° oven about 20 minutes or till golden. Remove from pans. Serve warm. Makes 24.

Refrigerated dinner rolls speed up putting together these extra-flaky two-bite morsels.

Beef Turnovers

½ pound ground beef ½ cup chopped cooked spinach, well-drained 1 3-ounce can chopped mushrooms, drained ¼ cup catsup ¼ teaspoon dried basil, crushed ¼ teaspoon dried thyme, crushed	● For filling, in a 10-inch skillet brown ground beef. Drain well. Stir in spinach, mushrooms, catsup, basil, thyme, and ¼ teaspoon *salt.* Set filling aside.
1 cup crushed onion toast crackers 1 cup all-purpose flour ¼ cup grated Parmesan cheese 6 tablespoons butter *or* margarine, softened 1 3-ounce package cream cheese, softened 4 to 5 tablespoons cold water	● For pastry, stir together crushed crackers, flour, and Parmesan cheese. Cut in butter or margarine and cream cheese till pieces are the size of small peas. Sprinkle *1 tablespoon* of the water over part of the mixture and gently toss with a fork. Repeat till all is moistened. Form dough into a ball.
1 beaten egg	● On a lightly floured surface, roll pastry to ⅛-inch thickness. Cut pastry into eighteen 4-inch circles, rerolling as necessary. Place *1 rounded tablespoon* of filling on *each* circle. Moisten edges with beaten egg. Fold pastry over filling to form a semicircle, then seal edges with the tines of a fork.
	● Place turnovers on a greased baking sheet. Brush with a little of the beaten egg. Bake in a 400° oven for 15 to 18 minutes or till golden brown. Serve warm. Makes 18.

Follow the old Boy Scout motto and "Be Prepared." Freeze the baked turnovers in foil and reheat them in the foil in a 375° oven for 10 to 12 minutes.

Baked Oysters

24 oysters in shells	● Thoroughly wash oysters in shells in cold water. Open shells with a blunt-tipped knife. Remove oysters from shells. Pat dry with paper towels. Discard upper shells. Wash deep bottom shells. Place each oyster in a shell half.	**Hang on to your oyster shells! If your seafood market doesn't have oysters-in-the-shell the next time you plan to prepare this showstopper, buy shucked oysters and recycle your shells.**
¼ cup chopped green onion 3 tablespoons butter *or* margarine ¾ cup finely crushed rich round crackers 2 tablespoons snipped parsley 1 tablespoon lemon juice ½ teaspoon dried oregano, crushed	● In a medium saucepan cook onion in butter or margarine till tender but not brown. Add crushed crackers, parsley, lemon juice, and oregano, then toss till combined. Top *each* oyster with about *2 teaspoons* of the crumb mixture.	
Rock salt *or* crumpled foil	● Line a shallow baking pan with rock salt or foil to about ½-inch depth. Arrange oysters in shells on salt. Bake in a 425° oven for 8 to 10 minutes or till crumb mixture is lightly browned. Serve immediately. Makes 6 to 8 servings.	

Calico Pastry Puffs

½ of a 17¼-ounce package (1 sheet) frozen puff pastry	● Let folded pastry stand at room temperature for 20 minutes. On a floured surface unfold pastry sheet. Roll out to a 10½-inch square. Cut into 1½-inch squares. Place squares on an ungreased baking sheet. Bake in a 425° oven for 12 minutes or till golden. Cool. Split each square in half horizontally.	**Our recipe tasters described these delicate pastry nips as "puffy little pillows."**
1 3-ounce package cream cheese, softened 3 tablespoons dairy sour cream 1 4½-ounce can tiny shrimp, rinsed, drained, and chopped 2 tablespoons finely chopped green pepper 2 tablespoons finely chopped pimiento 2 tablespoons snipped chives 2 tablespoons finely chopped ripe olives	● Meanwhile, combine cream cheese and sour cream. Stir in shrimp, green pepper, pimiento, chives, and olives.	
	● Spoon *1 teaspoon* shrimp mixture onto bottom of *each* square. Replace tops. Chill for 1 to 2 hours. Makes 49.	

Ricotta-Herb Tarts

½ of a 17¼-ounce package (1 sheet) frozen puff pastry
1 slightly beaten egg white
1 teaspoon water

● Let folded pastry stand at room temperature for 20 minutes to thaw. On a lightly floured surface unfold pastry and roll into a 15x10-inch rectangle. Cut rectangle in half lengthwise. Cut off two ¾-inch-wide strips crosswise, then two ¾-inch-wide strips lengthwise from *each* rectangle. Set the 8 pastry strips aside. (Cut decorative designs into pastry strips, if desired.)

Place the two rectangles on an ungreased baking sheet. Combine egg white and water. Brush rectangles with egg white mixture. Place 4 pastry strips atop edges of each rectangle, trimming to fit. (See photo, right.) Brush strips with egg white mixture. Prick bottom of pastry with a fork. Bake in a 375° oven for 10 minutes. Remove from oven.

Fresh dill or basil makes an elegant garnish for any appetizer—especially these eye-catching tarts.

Place the ¾-inch-wide pastry strips atop the rectangles to form a border and build up the sides. Trim strips to fit.

Ricotta Filling

● Spoon *half* of the Ricotta Filling into each partially baked pastry rectangle. Spread filling to edges. Return to the 375° oven and bake about 15 minutes more or till edges are golden. Cut rectangles crosswise. Serve warm. Makes 2 tarts (8 pieces each).

● **Ricotta Filling:** In a small mixer bowl combine 1 cup *ricotta cheese,* 1 *egg yolk,* 2 tablespoons grated *Parmesan cheese,* 2 tablespoons snipped *chives,* 1 tablespoon snipped *parsley,* 1 tablespoon *light cream or milk,* and ¼ teaspoon coarsely ground *black pepper.* Beat with an electric mixer till smooth.

Sausages in Whole Wheat Pastry

¾ cup whole wheat flour ½ cup all-purpose flour 1 teaspoon caraway seed ¼ teaspoon salt	● In a medium mixing bowl stir together flours, caraway seed, and salt.
⅓ cup shortening *or* lard 3 to 4 tablespoons cold milk	● Cut in shortening or lard till pieces are size of small peas. Sprinkle *1 tablespoon* of milk over part of the mixture, then toss gently with a fork. Push to side of bowl. Repeat till all is moistened. Form dough into a ball. On a lightly floured surface, flatten dough with your hands. Roll dough to ⅛-inch thickness. Cut out thirty-two 2-inch circles, rerolling scraps as necessary.
2 5½-ounce packages cocktail weiners *or* two 5-ounce packages small smoked sausage links Milk Horseradish-Mustard Sauce	● Wrap each circle around a weiner or sausage link. Place, seam side down, on a greased baking sheet. Brush with milk. Bake in a 400° oven about 15 minutes or till brown. Serve warm with Horseradish-Mustard Sauce. Makes 32.
	● **Horseradish-Mustard Sauce:** In a bowl stir together two 3-ounce packages *cream cheese, softened;* 3 tablespoons *milk;* and 2 tablespoons *horseradish mustard.* Makes about ¾ cup.

A host's greatest ally is an appetizer that can be made ahead and frozen. That's why you'll go for this contemporary version of "pigs in a blanket"— just reheat frozen appetizers in a 350° oven for 10 minutes.

Miniature Corn Puppies

1 cup all-purpose flour ⅔ cup yellow cornmeal 2 tablespoons sugar 1½ teaspoons baking powder ½ teaspoon salt 1 slightly beaten egg ¾ cup milk 2 tablespoons cooking oil	● For batter, in a medium mixing bowl stir together flour, cornmeal, sugar, baking powder, and salt. In a small mixing bowl combine egg, milk, and cooking oil. Add to dry ingredients, mixing well.
3 5½-ounce packages cocktail weiners, three 5-ounce packages small smoked sausage links, *or* 12 frankfurters, cut into 4 pieces Cooking oil for deep-fat frying	● Dip cocktail weiners, sausage links, or frankfurter pieces into batter. In a heavy saucepan fry weiners, a few at a time, in deep hot oil (375°) for 1½ to 2 minutes or till golden brown. Drain on paper towels. Serve warm. Makes about 48.

Don't be left in the kitchen frying these fritters while your guests are enjoying the party. Fry and freeze the appetizers before the fun begins, then reheat in a 450° oven about 10 minutes.

Meat and Melon Bites

1 **large honeydew melon** 1 **large cantaloupe** 1 **3-ounce package very thinly sliced ham** *or* **turkey**	● Cut melons in half and remove seeds. (*Or,* to prepare scalloped fruit bowl as in photo, see text at right.) Use a melon baller to scoop out pulp. Cut ham or turkey into 1-inch-wide strips.	**Fancy melon shells are an easy-to-make serving container.**
	● Wrap 1 strip of ham around *each* melon ball, then fasten with a toothpick.	Begin by cutting a very thin slice off the bottom of the melon so it sits flat. To make the decorative cut that's shown, insert a knife at a 45-degree angle through the rind slightly above the middle of the whole melon. Push the knife all the way through to the center. Then continue around the melon, cutting in saw-tooth manner.
Lettuce leaves	● Line 1 melon shell with lettuce leaves, then fill with wrapped melon balls. Makes about 60.	

Bull's-Eye Cheese Balls

1 cup shredded sharp cheddar cheese (4 ounces) ⅓ cup butter *or* margarine 1 cup all-purpose flour 1 teaspoon dry mustard ½ teaspoon paprika Dash ground red pepper	● For dough, bring cheese and butter to room temperature. Beat cheese and butter in a mixer bowl with an electric mixer till combined. In a small bowl mix flour, mustard, paprika, and red pepper. Stir flour mixture into cheese mixture till well combined, kneading in the last of the flour mixture by hand if necessary.
30 to 32 ripe *or* pimiento-stuffed olives	● Pat olives dry with paper towels. Wrap *1 rounded teaspoon* of dough around *each* olive, rolling it between your palms to make a smooth ball. Cover and chill balls about 1 hour.
	● Place balls on an ungreased baking sheet. Bake in a 400° oven for 12 to 15 minutes or till golden brown. Serve warm. Makes 30 to 32.

These cheddar-flavored morsels can be stuffed with a lot more than olives. Try using canned medium shrimp (rinse and drain before using), pickle chunks, or frankfurters or smoked sausage links (cut into ½-inch pieces). *Or,* for a really rich tidbit, stuff them with a cashew, walnut, or macadamia nut.

Cheese and Spinach Puffs

1 10-ounce package frozen chopped spinach ½ cup chopped onion	● In a saucepan combine spinach and onion. Cook according to spinach package directions. Drain well, pressing out excess liquid.
2 slightly beaten eggs ½ cup grated Parmesan cheese (2 ounces) ½ cup shredded cheddar cheese (2 ounces) ½ cup blue cheese salad dressing ¼ cup butter *or* margarine, melted ⅛ teaspoon garlic powder 1 8½-ounce package corn muffin mix	● In a medium bowl combine eggs, cheeses, salad dressing, butter or margarine, and garlic powder. Stir in muffin mix and spinach mixture till well combined. Cover and chill thoroughly. Shape spinach mixture into 1-inch balls. Cover and chill till serving time. (*Or,* place balls in a freezer container. Seal, label, and freeze.)
	● Before serving, place balls on a baking sheet. Bake chilled balls in a 350° oven for 10 to 12 minutes or till light brown. (Bake frozen balls for 12 to 15 minutes.) Serve warm. Nibkes about 60.

Your guests are bound to give these tidbits a four-star rating.

Mini Drums with Honey-Orange Sauce

24 chicken wings

● For mini drumsticks (see photos, right and below), bend the 2 larger sections of each chicken wing back and forth, breaking the cartilage that connects the larger wing portion (the mini drumstick) with the 2-part wing-tip section. Use a knife or cleaver to cut through the skin and cartilage that connects the 2 larger sections of each wing. Reserve 2-part wing-tip section to make stock or soup.

● Use a small knife to cut cartilage loose from the cut end of each mini drumstick. Push meat and skin to top of bone, shaping it into a compact ball.

● Place mini drumsticks, meat end down, in a 13x9x2-inch baking pan. Bake in a 350° oven for 20 to 25 minutes.

2 teaspoons cornstarch
½ cup orange juice
1 tablespoon honey
1 tablespoon dry white wine
1 tablespoon soy sauce
1 tablespoon butter *or* margarine
Orange wedges (optional)
Parsley sprigs (optional)

● Meanwhile, for sauce, in a medium saucepan stir cornstarch into orange juice, then stir in honey, wine, and soy sauce. Cook and stir till thickened and bubbly, then cook and stir for 2 minutes more. Stir in butter or margarine till melted. Brush chicken with sauce during the last 10 minutes of baking and again just before serving. Garnish with orange wedges and parsley, if desired. Makes 24.

Pictured on page 62.

Flex the mini drumstick section and the 2-part wing-tip section of each chicken wing between your hands to break the cartilage that connects them. Then use a sharp knife to cut through the skin and cartilage. (Save the 2-part wing-tip section for stock or soup.)

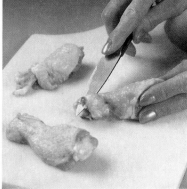

Use the tip of a sharp knife to cut the cartilage around the bone loose from the cut end of the mini drumstick.

Push the meat and skin of the mini drumstick to the top of the bone, making a compact ball.

Personality Pizzas

2 packages (10 each) refrigerated biscuits	
1 15½-ounce jar pizza sauce	
Ground Beef and Mushroom Topper	
Pepperoni Topper	
Mexicali Topper	

● Separate biscuits, then cut each one in half. Roll each half into a ball. Flatten balls into 2- to 2½-inch circles on an ungreased baking sheet. Spread about *1 heaping teaspoon* pizza sauce over *each* biscuit, spreading to within ¼ inch of edge. Add desired topper. Bake in a 425° oven for 10 to 12 minutes or till golden brown. Serve warm. Makes 40.

● **Ground Beef and Mushroom Topper:** Cook ½ pound *ground beef* and ½ cup chopped *onion* till meat is browned. Drain off fat. Drain two 4-ounce cans *sliced mushrooms*, and stir into ground beef. Top flattened biscuits with beef mixture and 1 cup shredded *mozzarella cheese*.

● **Pepperoni Topper:** Place 1 thin slice *pepperoni* on each flattened biscuit. Top biscuits with 1 cup sliced *green pepper* and 1 cup shredded *cheddar cheese*.

● **Mexicali Topper:** Top flattened biscuits with one 4½-ounce can *sliced pitted ripe olives* (about ½ cup) and 1 cup shredded *mozzarella or hot pepper cheese*.

Don't be caught offguard when unexpected guests ring your doorbell. Bake a bunch of these miniature pizzas, store them in your freezer, and surprise your guests with a quick snack. Pop as many individual pizzas as needed into a 350° oven for 9 to 10 minutes.

Sherried Onions and Olives

½ cup dry sherry
¼ cup red wine vinegar
2 tablespoons cooking oil
½ teaspoon dried oregano, crushed
½ teaspoon dried basil, crushed
1 clove garlic, minced
1 cup frozen small whole onions
1 6-ounce can pitted ripe olives, drained
1 2½-ounce jar pimiento-stuffed olives, drained

● For marinade, in a medium bowl combine sherry, wine vinegar, oil, oregano, basil, and garlic. Add onions and olives to marinade, stirring gently. Cover and chill for 1 to 3 days, stirring occasionally. Before serving, use a slotted spoon to remove onions and olives from marinade. Makes about 3 cups.

Our taste panel really liked the slightly stronger sherry flavor (especially in the green olives) that came through after marinating 3 days.

Everyone Likes 'Em Hot!

How to keep hot foods hot is a problem that party givers are always trying to solve.

The answer doesn't require a maid or a magician—just heat one round of appetizers at a time, if possible. This way, another batch of hot appetizers will be coming from the oven just as the last batch is eaten. Or if you own one, use an electric appliance to keep appetizers hot once they're cooked. An electric skillet, hot tray, griddle, or bun warmer will do the trick.

Cheese Ribbons

1½ cups shredded American *or* cheddar cheese (6 ounces)
½ cup butter *or* margarine
1 egg
2 teaspoons prepared mustard
⅛ teaspoon garlic powder
1¾ cups all-purpose flour

● For dough, in a mixer bowl beat cheese and butter or margarine together with an electric mixer. Add egg, mustard, and garlic powder, then beat well. Stir in flour till well combined, kneading in the last of the flour by hand if necessary.

● Using the ribbon plate of a cookie press, press dough onto an ungreased baking sheet into long strips. Score strips diagonally every 3 to 4 inches. Bake in a 375° oven for 10 to 12 minutes or till lightly browned. Remove from baking sheet immediately. Cool on a wire rack. Break along score marks. Serve warm or cool. Makes about 40.

Maybe the only time you use a cookie press is to make rich and buttery spritz cookies. Well, dig it out of the closet for these savory, cheese-flavored snacks. They're shaped using the ribbon plate of a cookie press.

Pepper and Cheese Squares

½ cup all-purpose flour
1 teaspoon baking powder
½ teaspoon salt
8 eggs
3 cups shredded Monterey Jack cheese (12 ounces)
1½ cups cream-style cottage cheese
3 *or* 4 pickled jalapeño peppers, rinsed and chopped (about 2 tablespoons)
2 tablespoons chopped pimiento
2 tablespoons sliced, pitted ripe olives

● In a bowl stir together flour, baking powder, and salt, then set aside. In large mixer bowl beat eggs with an electric mixer till well combined. Stir flour mixture into beaten eggs and mix well. Fold in Monterey Jack cheese, cottage cheese, peppers, pimiento, and olives.

All the ingredients of a quiche, without the fuss of a crust.

Tortilla chips (optional)

● Pour into a greased 13x9x2-inch baking dish. Bake in a 350° oven about 40 minutes or till set and golden brown. Let stand 10 minutes. Cut into about 1½-inch squares. Serve warm on tortilla chips, if desired. Makes about 48.

Mini Drums with Honey-Orange Sauce
(see recipe, page 57)

Maple-Syrup Appetizer Meatballs

Golden Glazed Chinese Ribs

Maple-Syrup Appetizer Meatballs

1 beaten egg
½ cup milk
½ cup cornbread stuffing mix
¼ cup finely chopped celery
1 teaspoon dry mustard
¾ pound ground fully cooked ham
½ pound ground pork

● In a large bowl combine egg and milk. Stir in stuffing mix, celery, mustard, and dash *pepper*. Let stand 3 minutes. Add ham and pork. Mix well. Shape into 1-inch meatballs. Place in a shallow baking pan. Bake in a 350° oven for 15 to 18 minutes or till done. Drain well.

Cook these meatballs ahead and freeze them for an impromptu party. Then reheat the frozen meatballs right in the sauce.

2 cups bias-sliced carrots *or* bite-size cauliflower flowerets
1 cup maple-flavored syrup
½ cup vinegar
2 teaspoons dry mustard
2 tablespoons cornstarch
2 tablespoons water
1 green pepper, cut into strips

● Meanwhile, in a medium saucepan cook carrots or cauliflower, covered, in a small amount of boiling water for 10 to 15 minutes or till tender. Drain well. In the same saucepan combine syrup, vinegar, and mustard. Combine cornstarch and water. Add carrots, cornstarch mixture, and green pepper to syrup mixture. Cook and stir till thickened and bubbly, then cook and stir 2 minutes more. Add meatballs. Heat through. Serve warm. Makes about 50.

In a saucepan combine syrup, vinegar, and dry mustard. Bring to boiling and add frozen meatballs. Cover and simmer for 8 to 10 minutes. At the same time, cook vegetables and combine cornstarch and water. Stir cooked vegetables, green pepper, and cornstarch mixture into syrup mixture. Cook and serve as directed at left.

Golden Glazed Chinese Ribs

2 pounds meaty pork spareribs *or* loin back ribs, sawed in half across the bones
1 tablespoon sugar
¼ teaspoon paprika
¼ teaspoon ground turmeric
⅛ teaspoon celery seed
Dash dry mustard

● Cut ribs into single-rib portions. Rinse and pat dry with paper towels. In a small bowl combine sugar, paprika, turmeric, celery seed, and mustard. Rub ribs thoroughly with sugar mixture. Cover and let stand for 1 hour at room temperature or 4 to 6 hours in refrigerator. Place ribs, meaty side down, in a foil-lined large shallow roasting pan. Bake, uncovered, in a 450° oven for 30 minutes. Drain off fat. Turn meaty side up. Reduce heat to 350° and bake for 15 minutes more.

Ask your butcher to saw the ribs in half across the bones—it makes them easier to handle as appetizers.

½ cup water
¼ cup snipped dried apricots
2 tablespoons corn syrup
2 teaspoons vinegar
1 teaspoon lemon juice
¼ teaspoon ground ginger

● Meanwhile, in a saucepan combine water, apricots, corn syrup, vinegar, lemon juice, and ginger. Bring to boiling. Reduce heat. Cover and simmer for 5 minutes. Cool slightly. Pour mixture into a blender container or food processor bowl. Cover and process till smooth.

To make green onion brushes for a garnish, trim green onions at both ends. Cut thin 2-inch slits at one or both ends. Place in ice water to crisp and curl the ends.

Lettuce leaves
Green onion brushes (optional)

● Drain off fat. Brush ribs with apricot mixture. Bake 15 minutes more. Brush just before serving. Serve on a lettuce-lined platter. Garnish with green onion brushes, if desired. Makes 6 servings.

Chicken-Stuffed Cream Puffs

½ cup water
¼ cup butter *or* margarine
½ cup all-purpose flour

● For dough, in a medium saucepan bring water and butter or margarine to boiling. Add flour and stir vigorously. Cook and stir till mixture forms a ball that doesn't separate. Remove from heat and cool 5 minutes.

A word to the wise: Bake these puffs ahead so they're ready when you need them. Then store them tightly covered at room temperature up to 24 hours. (Or, freeze them in moisture- and vaporproof wrap for up to two weeks.) Come party time—fill and enjoy!

2 eggs
½ cup shredded Muenster *or* Swiss cheese (2 ounces)

● Add eggs, one at a time, beating 1 minute after each or till smooth. Stir in shredded cheese.

Cottage Cheese-Shrimp Filling
Chicken-Mushroom Filling

● Using *1 rounded teaspoon* dough for *each* puff, drop dough onto a greased baking sheet. Bake in a 400° oven about 20 minutes or till puffed and golden brown. Remove from oven and cut off tops. Remove any soft dough. Cool puffs on a wire rack. Before serving, fill puff bottoms with desired filling and replace tops. Makes 30.

Once the puffs are filled, they'll keep for up to 4 hours in the refrigerator without getting soggy.

● **Cottage Cheese-Shrimp Filling:** In a bowl combine two 4¼-ounce cans tiny *shrimp,* rinsed and drained; ½ cup plain *yogurt;* ½ cup small-curd *cottage cheese,* drained; ¼ cup finely chopped *celery;* ¼ cup shredded *carrot;* 2 tablespoons sliced *green onion;* 1 *hard-cooked egg,* chopped; and ¼ teaspoon *dried dillweed.* Cover and chill.

● **Chicken-Mushroom Filling:** In a bowl combine one 5-ounce can *chunk-style chicken,* drained and flaked; ½ cup finely chopped *water chestnuts;* ¼ cup *buttermilk salad dressing with chives;* one 2½-ounce jar *sliced mushrooms,* drained and chopped; 1 tablespoon chopped *pimiento;* ¼ teaspoon *dry mustard;* and dash *salt.* Cover and chill.

Marinated Mushrooms

1½ cups water
½ cup olive *or* salad oil
½ cup dry white wine
8 whole black peppers
3 tablespoons lemon juice
1 teaspoon dried thyme, crushed
¾ teaspoon coriander seed
¾ teaspoon salt
1½ pounds fresh whole mushrooms

● For marinade, in a 12-inch skillet combine water, oil, wine, black pepper, lemon juice, thyme, coriander, and salt. Bring to boiling, then add mushrooms. Reduce heat and simmer, covered, for 5 to 10 minutes or till mushrooms are just tender. Use a slotted spoon to remove mushrooms from marinade to a bowl.

For an elegant touch, crown a plate of these herb-marinated mushrooms with a dazzling lemon rose.

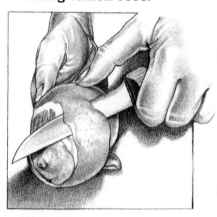

Bibb *or* iceberg lettuce

● Bring marinade to boiling. Boil hard for 10 minutes or till reduced to 1½ cups. Pour marinade over mushrooms. Cover bowl and chill several hours or overnight, stirring occasionally. Before serving, use a slotted spoon to transfer mushrooms to a lettuce-lined plate. Makes 8 servings.

Using a medium lemon, cut a "base" from one end of the lemon (do not sever). Continue cutting one continuous narrow strip in spiral fashion, using a sawing motion. Taper the end to a point as you remove the peel from the fruit. Curl the strip onto its base in the shape of an open rose.

Pepperoni-Mustard Twists

2 tablespoons finely chopped onion
2 tablespoons Dijon-style mustard
1 tablespoon snipped parsley
1 teaspoon poppy seed

● In a small bowl combine onion, mustard, parsley, and poppy seed.

The herbs, spices, and white wine that give French-style Dijon mustard its special flavor add a pleasant tang to these pastry snacks.

1 package (8) refrigerated crescent rolls
½ cup chopped pepperoni

● Unroll and separate crescent rolls into triangles. Spread some of the onion-mustard mixture over each triangle, then sprinkle with pepperoni. Roll up according to package directions.

● Place on an ungreased baking sheet, seam side down. Bake in a 375° oven for 10 to 13 minutes or till lightly browned. Serve warm. Makes 8.

Totable Tidbits

Tired of going to potluck parties with hot appetizers that turn cold before you get out of the house? Fret no more—this selection of recipes was developed with that very problem in mind. These recipes won't fall apart, fall down, get cold, or run together as you're transporting them to your party site. Turn to pages 68 and 69 for recipes.

MENU
Cheddar Crock
Stuffed Bread Rolls
Tarragon Tidbits

Stuffed Bread Rolls

Pictured on pages 66–67.

8	slices bacon
2	teaspoons unflavored gelatin
¼	cup cold water

● For filling, cook bacon in a 10-inch skillet till crisp. Drain, reserving 2 tablespoons drippings. Crumble bacon and set aside. Soften gelatin in cold water for 5 minutes.

1	pound fresh mushrooms, chopped
1	cup chopped green onion
2	cloves garlic, minced
¼	cup dry white *or* red wine
2	teaspoons basil
¼	teaspoon salt
¼	teaspoon bottled hot pepper sauce

● Meanwhile, cook mushrooms, green onion, and garlic in reserved bacon drippings till tender. Remove from heat. Add wine, basil, salt, and hot pepper sauce. Cook and stir over medium-high heat about 5 minutes or till most of liquid has evaporated. Reduce heat and add softened gelatin. Cook and stir over low heat till gelatin is dissolved.

| 1 | cup whipping cream |
| ¼ | cup snipped parsley |

● Place mushroom mixture in a blender container or food processor bowl. Cover and process till almost smooth. Cool to room temperature. Whip cream till soft peaks form (tips curl), then fold into mushroom mixture with crumbled bacon and parsley.

| 4 | French-style rolls (about 8 inches long) |

● Cut a ¼- to ½-inch-thick slice from bottoms of rolls. Set aside. Hollow out rolls, leaving a ½-inch-thick shell (save bread trimmings for another use). Spoon filling into roll shells. Replace bottom slice of rolls. Wrap and chill overnight. Before serving, cut into 1-inch slices. Serves 6 to 8.

MENU COUNTDOWN
2 Days Ahead:
Prepare Cheddar Crock and refrigerate. Prepare Tarragon Tidbits and refrigerate.
1 Day Ahead:
Prepare Stuffed Bread Rolls and refrigerate.
Day of Party:
Prepare the foods for transporting. Drain Tarragon Tidbits, then put the vegetables into a nonbreakable bowl and cover. Wrap Stuffed Bread Rolls tightly in foil. Pack all chilled foods into a cooler. Remember to take a knife and crackers for the Cheddar Crock. You'll also need paper plates and plastic forks for the vegetables. If you like, take along some decorative cocktail napkins, too.

Cheddar Crock

Pictured on pages 66–67.

1½ cups shredded cheddar
    cheese (6 ounces)
1 3-ounce package cream
    cheese
¼ cup butter *or* margarine
⅓ cup milk
1 tablespoon chopped green
    onion
½ teaspoon Dijon-style
    mustard
¼ teaspoon Worcestershire
    sauce
    Few dashes bottled hot
    pepper sauce
    Assorted crackers

● Bring cheeses and butter or margarine to room temperature. In a small mixer bowl beat chesses and butter or margarine with an electric mixer till combined. Add milk, green onion, mustard, Worcestershire sauce, and hot pepper sauce. Beat till smooth. Pack into a 16-ounce crock or jar. Refrigerate at least 6 hours. Serve at room temperature with crackers. Makes about 2 cups.

By the time you get the cheese spread to your party destination, it will be like whipped butter— just the right spreading consistency.

Tarragon Tidbits

Pictured on pages 66–67.

1 carrot, cut into 2-inch
    sticks
1 cup broccoli *or*
    cauliflower flowerets
1 small zucchini, cut into
    sticks
1 small cucumber, halved
    and thinly sliced
1 small onion, thinly sliced
    and separated into rings

● In a small saucepan cook carrots, covered, in a small amount of water for 2 minutes. Add broccoli or cauliflower flowerets and bring to boiling. Reduce heat and simmer about 3 minutes or till crisp-tender. Drain well. In a large bowl combine cooked and drained vegetables, zucchini, cucumber, and onion.

Marinate the veggies with red or white wine vinegar—the tarragon flavor is great with either one.

⅓ cup wine vinegar
¼ cup cooking oil
2 tablespoons water
2 cloves garlic, minced
1 teaspoon dried tarragon,
    crushed

● In a screw-top jar combine vinegar, cooking oil, water, garlic, and tarragon. Cover and shake well, then pour over vegetables. Cover and chill at least 6 hours or overnight, stirring occasionally. Drain well before serving. Serves 6 to 8.

Blueberry Bites

½ cup butter *or* margarine, softened
1 3-ounce package cream cheese, softened
1 cup all-purpose flour

● For tart shells, in a small mixer bowl beat together butter or margarine and cream cheese. Add flour and beat well. Cover and chill dough about 1 hour.

In a hurry? Skip making the blueberry filling. With the variety of canned pie fillings available, there are lots of other tarts you can prepare. Cherry, raisin, strawberry, and red raspberry are just a few of the possibilities.

2 tablespoons brown sugar
1 tablespoon cornstarch
2 cups fresh *or* frozen blueberries, thawed
2 teaspoons lemon juice

● Meanwhile, for blueberry filling, in a medium saucepan combine brown sugar and cornstarch. Mash blueberries slightly, then add blueberries and lemon juice to saucepan. Cook and stir till thickened and bubbly, then cook and stir for 2 minutes more. Remove from heat. Cover with waxed paper. Cool.

Whipped cream (optional)

● Divide dough into 24 balls. Place each ball in an ungreased 1¾-inch muffin cup. Press dough evenly against bottom and sides of cup. (See photo, below.) Fill *each* pastry-lined muffin cup with about *2 teaspoons* of blueberry filling. Bake in a 325° oven for 20 to 25 minutes or till lightly browned. Cool slightly. Remove from pan. Cool completely on a wire rack. Just before serving, dollop with whipped cream, if desired. Makes 24.

Be sure to press the dough *evenly* against bottoms and sides of the muffin cups. If the dough is too thin at any one place, the tarts may crack as they bake and allow the filling to leak through.

Brandy Tarts

½ cup butter *or* margarine, softened
1 3-ounce package cream cheese, softened
1 cup all-purpose flour

● For tart shells, in a small mixer bowl beat together butter or margarine and cream cheese. Add flour and beat well. Cover and chill dough about 1 hour.

Here's a great make-ahead idea: Wrap and freeze the petite cream cheese tart shells after they're baked and cooled. Then pull them out of the freezer just before you're ready to make the filling.

● Divide dough into 24 balls. Place each ball in an ungreased 1¾-inch muffin cup. Press dough evenly against bottom and sides of cup. (See photo, left.) Bake in a 325° oven for 20 to 25 minutes or till lightly browned. Cool slightly. Remove from pan. Cool completely on a wire rack.

1 package 4-serving-size *instant* chocolate *or* vanilla pudding mix
2 tablespoons brandy
1 tablespoon crème de cacao
½ of a 4-ounce container frozen whipped dessert topping, thawed

● Meanwhile, for filling, prepare pudding mix according to package directions, *except* use 1 cup milk. Stir in brandy and crème de cacao. Fold dessert topping into pudding mixture.

¼ cup chopped pistachios *or* pecans

● Spoon filling into cooled tart shells. Sprinkle with nuts. Chill thoroughly. Makes 24.

Fruited Rum Balls

1½ cups crushed graham
      crackers (about 20
      graham cracker squares)
  1 6-ounce package
      mixed dried fruit bits
      (1½ cups)
  1 cup chopped pecans
  1 7-ounce jar marshmallow
      creme
⅓ cup rum
  1 teaspoon finely shredded
      lemon peel
¼ teaspoon ground
      cinnamon
¼ teaspoon ground nutmeg

● In a bowl stir together graham crackers, dried fruit bits, and pecans. Set aside. In a 1-quart saucepan combine marshmallow creme, rum, lemon peel, cinnamon, and nutmeg. Cook and stir over low heat till marshmallow creme is melted and mixture is well combined. Pour over dried fruit mixture, stirring till well combined. Cover and chill for 2 or 3 hours or till firm.

This fruit mixture is a little sticky even after chilling, so you'll find the balls easier to shape if you first moisten your hands with water.

  1 cup coconut

● Shape chilled fruit mixture into 1-inch balls, then roll in coconut. Wrap fruit balls individually in plastic wrap. Store in an airtight container. (Balls can be frozen for up to 6 months.) Makes about 42.

Apricot Dessert Dip

½ cup dried apricots
  1 cup water

● In a small saucepan simmer apricots, covered, in water about 15 minutes or till tender. Drain, reserving ¼ cup liquid.

Looking for a light-yet-easy dessert? This creamy dip, along with some fresh fruit, fits your needs perfectly.

  1 tablespoon sugar
  1 3-ounce package cream
      cheese, cut up
½ cup dairy sour cream
⅛ teaspoon ground nutmeg
      Assorted fruit dippers
      such as apple wedges,
      pear slices, pineapple
      chunks, and whole
      strawberries

● In a blender container or food processor bowl combine sugar, apricots, and reserved liquid. Cover and process till smooth. Add cream cheese, sour cream, and nutmeg. Cover and process till smooth. Spoon apricot mixture into a bowl. Cover and chill. Serve with fruit dippers. Makes 1⅓ cups.

Chocolate-Almond Macaroons

2 egg whites
½ teaspoon almond extract
⅔ cup sugar
2 tablespoons unsweetened cocoa powder
1 3½-ounce can (1⅓ cups) flaked coconut
½ cup finely chopped almonds

● Grease a cookie sheet. Set aside. In a mixer bowl beat egg whites and almond extract with an electric mixer till soft peaks form (tips curl). In a small bowl stir together sugar and cocoa powder. Gradually add sugar-cocoa powder mixture to egg whites, beating till stiff peaks form (tips stand straight). Fold in coconut and almonds.

Melted chocolate (optional)

● Drop from a teaspoon 1½ inches apart onto prepared cookie sheet. Bake in a 325° oven about 15 minutes or till cookies are dry and crisp. Cool on a wire rack. Drizzle with melted chocolate, if desired. Makes about 42.

Cap off any occasion in style by serving these light and crunchy cookies with the Spiced Dessert Coffee on page 90.

Easy Walnut Penuche

Butter *or* margarine
6 tablespoons butter *or* margarine
1 cup packed brown sugar
¼ cup milk

● Line an 8x8x2-inch baking pan with foil, extending foil over edges of pan. Butter the foil, then set the pan aside. In a small saucepan melt the 6 tablespoons butter or margarine, then stir in brown sugar. Cook over low heat for 2 minutes, stirring constantly. Increase heat to medium and add milk. Cook and stir till mixture boils. Remove pan from heat and cool for 30 minutes.

2½ cups sifted powdered sugar
1 cup chopped walnuts

● Stir the melted butter mixture into the powdered sugar. Stir in chopped nuts. Turn penuche into prepared pan. While penuche is warm, score it into 1-inch squares. Chill several hours or till firm. Use foil to lift candy out of pan, then cut candy into squares. Makes about 1½ pounds or 64 pieces.

In the candy world, penuche (puh-NOO-chee) refers to a fudge made with brown sugar.

Instead of squares, try cutting this fudge into different shapes using hors d'oeuvre or small cookie cutters.

Fluffy Fruit Dip

1 5½-ounce can pear nectar
2 teaspoons cornstarch
1 tablespoon honey
¼ teaspoon lemon peel

● In a small saucepan combine pear nectar and cornstarch. Stir in honey and lemon peel. Cook and stir over medium heat till thickened and bubbly, then cook and stir for 2 minutes more.

½ cup plain yogurt
⅓ cup mayonnaise *or* salad dressing
  Assorted fruit dippers (see suggestions at right)

● Remove from heat and cool. Stir in yogurt and mayonnaise or salad dressing. Transfer to a serving bowl. Cover and chill for several hours or overnight. Serve with fruit dippers. Makes about 1⅓ cups.

Fresh fruit and Fluffy Fruit Dip make an irresistible duo. Take your pick from apple wedges, bias-sliced bananas, pineapple chunks, pear slices, melon balls, whole strawberries, or cherries. Brush the apple wedges, banana slices, and pear slices with lemon juice to keep them from browning.

Orange Cream Cheese Spread

1 8-ounce package cream cheese, softened
1 tablespoon sugar
1 tablespoon orange liqueur
1½ teaspoons finely shredded orange peel
  Assorted sliced breads (see suggestions at right)

● In a small mixer bowl combine cream cheese, sugar, orange liqueur, and orange peel. Beat with an electric mixer on low speed till well combined. Cover and chill for several hours or overnight. Serve at room temperature with breads. Makes about 1 cup.

This rich spread is tops on everything from toasted English muffins to bagels to Boston brown bread to banana nut bread.

Marzipan

1	cup blanched whole almonds (6 ounces) *or* 1⅓ cups slivered almonds	● Place almonds in a blender container or food processor bowl. Cover and process till ground.
1⅓	cups sifted powdered sugar	● In a mixer bowl beat together ground almonds, 1⅓ cups powdered sugar, water, and almond extract with an electric mixer till mixture forms a ball. Beat in 2¼ cups powdered sugar. Stir in enough beaten egg white to form a claylike mixture. Tint with food coloring, if desired.
2	tablespoons water	
½	teaspoon almond extract	
2¼	cups sifted powdered sugar	
1	tablespoon slightly beaten egg white	
	Few drops desired food coloring (optional)	
	Powdered sugar	● Mold in mint molds dusted with powdered sugar or shape by hand as desired. Store, covered, at room temperature. Makes 32 to 40 candies.

These exquisite fondant-like candies made with almond paste can be molded in mint molds or shaped by hand.

Fancy Fruit

5 to 6 cups maraschino cherries with stems, canned mandarin orange sections, fresh dark sweet cherries, fresh strawberries, *and/or* dried fruits	● Drain cherries, oranges, and strawberries thoroughly on paper towels for several hours.	**Dip the fruit pieces into the melted chocolate with your fingers, not a fork or a toothpick, because piercing or squeezing the fruit can cause juices to drip into the chocolate and make it clump.**
1 pound dipping chocolate *or* confectioners' coating	● Melt the dipping chocolate or confectioners' coating (if using chocolate, see tip below). Using your fingers, hold fruit by one end and dip a portion of it into melted chocolate. Let excess chocolate drip off.	
1 cup finely chopped pistachios, pecans, *or* almonds	● Dip chocolate-coated fruit into chopped nuts. (See photo, right.) Place fruit on a baking sheet lined with waxed paper and chill till firm. Serve fruit the same day it is dipped. Makes about 2 pounds.	**Dip chocolate-coated fruit into a small bowl of chopped nuts. Use your fingers to help coat fruit, if necessary.**

Tempering Chocolate

The secret of professional-looking dipped candies and fruit is tempering (melting and cooling) chocolate to the right dipping temperature.

Why temper chocolate? As chocolate melts, the cocoa butter separates from the liquid. Then, as the mixture cools, the cocoa butter blends back in. Without tempering, the surface of the chocolate will speckle or develop gray streaks as it hardens.

Here's how to temper chocolate. Dip candies or fruit on a cool, dry day (60° to 65°). Use 1 to 1½ pounds of chocolate for dipping. (Less than 1 pound is hard to work with and more than 2 pounds is difficult to keep evenly

melted.) Finely chop the chocolate. Fill the bottom of a double boiler with water to within ½ inch of the upper pan. Make sure the upper pan does not touch the water, or the chocolate may overheat. Bring the water to boiling and remove from the heat. Place about *one-fourth* of chocolate in the top of the double boiler, then set over hot water till chocolate begins to melt. Add the remaining chocolate, about ½ cup at a time, *stirring constantly* after each addition till it is melted. Stir till chocolate reaches 120°.

If necessary to help chocolate reach 120°, reheat water. (Use care not to let any water splash into the

chocolate, or the chocolate will thicken and be unusable for dipping.) After the chocolate has reached 120°, refill the bottom of the double boiler with *cool* water to within ½ inch of the upper pan. Place chocolate over cool water. *Stir frequently* till the chocolate cools to 83°.

Now begin dipping the candies or fruit. Work quickly, stirring chocolate frequently to keep it evenly heated. The chocolate will stay close to 83° about 30 minutes. If the chocolate cools to below 80°, retemper it.

Apricot Burritos

1 cup water
1 6-ounce package dried
   apricots, snipped
¼ cup sugar
¼ cup packed brown sugar
¼ teaspoon ground
   cinnamon
¼ teaspoon ground nutmeg
	● In a small saucepan combine water, apricots, sugar, brown sugar, cinnamon, and nutmeg. Bring to boiling. Reduce heat. Simmer, uncovered, for 10 to 15 minutes or till fruit is tender and mixture is thickened, stirring occasionally. Cool.

20 to 25 6-inch flour tortillas	● To assemble, spoon about *1 tablespoon* of the apricot mixture along one edge of *each* tortilla. Roll tortilla up. Keep tortillas covered with a damp towel before and after filling.
Cooking oil for deep-fat frying	● In a heavy 12-inch skillet heat about ¾ inch cooking oil to 350°. Place 5 tortillas, seam side down, in hot oil. Cook about 2 minutes or till golden, turning once. Drain tortillas on paper towels. Repeat with remaining tortillas. Serve warm or cool. Makes 20 to 25.

Make life a little easier—cook these dessert burritos in an electric skillet. It regulates the temperature of the oil automatically, so you don't have to fuss with a thermometer.

Easy Chocolate Crunchies

1 14-ounce can (1¼ cups)
   *sweetened condensed
   milk*
1 6-ounce package (1 cup)
   semisweet chocolate
   pieces
1 6-ounce package (1 cup)
   butterscotch pieces
½ teaspoon vanilla
	● In a large saucepan cook and stir milk, chocolate pieces, and butterscotch pieces over low heat till melted. Remove from heat and stir in vanilla.

3 cups broken pretzel
   sticks
1 cup peanuts
1 3-ounce can (2½ cups)
   chow mein noodles
	● In a large bowl combine pretzels, peanuts, and chow mein noodles. Stir into melted chocolate mixture. Drop from a teaspoon onto a baking sheet lined with waxed paper. Cover and chill till firm. Store tightly covered in the refrigerator. Makes about 72.

This "melt-'n'-mix" candy comes in handy for those hectic days when the minute hand races around the clock.

Buckeye Drops

1¼ cups sifted powdered
      sugar
1   cup peanut butter
3   tablespoons butter *or*
      margarine, softened
½   teaspoon vanilla

● In a medium bowl stir together powdered sugar, peanut butter, butter or margarine, and vanilla till well combined. Shape mixture into 1-inch balls.

These candies get their name because they resemble the large, nutlike seeds of a buckeye tree. According to legend, good luck comes to those who carry the inedible seeds.

1   6-ounce package (1 cup)
      semisweet chocolate
      pieces
2   teaspoons shortening

● In a medium saucepan melt chocolate pieces and shortening over low heat. Remove pan from heat. Dip peanut butter balls into melted chocolate, leaving about one-third of the peanut butter showing on top. (See photo, below.) Let excess chocolate drip off. Place dipped balls on a baking sheet lined with waxed paper. Chill till firm. Store tightly covered in refrigerator. Makes about 36.

Using a fork, dip a peanut butter ball into the melted chocolate. Lift the ball out and draw the fork across the rim of the pan to remove excess chocolate. Place the dipped ball on waxed paper. (If a lot of chocolate pools at the base of the peanut butter ball, next time let more chocolate drip off your fork.)

Cocktail Party for 12 or 24

Cocktail parties are always "in" because they're a simple and informal way to entertain lots of people without a lot of work. Whether you're welcoming new neighbors to the block, celebrating a promotion, or just enjoying an evening with friends, you'll find making this menu (see recipes, pages 82–85) is fun. What's more, you'll be amazed how easily the foods go together—whether your gathering is for 12 or 24.

MENU
Barbecued Mini Drums
Smoky Cheese Log
Avocado Dip
Sangria Sipper

MENU COUNTDOWN
1 Week Ahead:
Prepare Smoky Cheese Log and freeze.
1 Day Ahead:
Remove Smoky Cheese Log from freezer and thaw in refrigerator.
4 Hours Ahead:
Combine wine and iced tea mix for Sangria Sipper. Add orange and lemon slices and refrigerate. Prepare Avocado Dip and vegetable dippers and refrigerate.

1½ Hours Ahead:
Prepare Barbecued Mini Drums.
Just Before Party:
Stir carbonated water into Sangria Sipper. Garnish with lemon slices, wedges, or both.

Barbecued Chicken Wings

Pictured on pages 80–81.

For 12

For 24

12 chicken wings (about 2 pounds)

● Cut off and discard tips of chicken wings. Cut wings at joints to form 24 (or 48) pieces. Place the 24 chicken wing pieces in a single layer in an ungreased 13x9x2-inch baking pan. (Use a 15x10x1-inch shallow baking pan for 48 pieces.) Bake in a 375° oven for 20 minutes. Drain well.

24 chicken wings (about 4 pounds)

¼ cup catsup
2 tablespoons water
2 tablespoons finely chopped onion
1 tablespoon cooking oil
1½ teaspoons vinegar
1 teaspoon brown sugar
1 teaspoon Worcestershire sauce
¼ teaspoon dried oregano, crushed
¼ teaspoon chili powder
¼ teaspoon dry mustard
1 bay leaf
1 clove garlic, minced

● Meanwhile, for barbecue sauce, in a saucepan combine catsup, water, onion, cooking oil, vinegar, brown sugar, Worcestershire sauce, oregano, chili powder, mustard, bay leaf, and garlic. Bring mixture to boiling, then reduce heat. Simmer, covered, for 10 minutes, stirring occasionally. Discard bay leaf.

½ cup catsup
¼ cup water
¼ cup finely chopped onion
2 tablespoons cooking oil
1 tablespoon vinegar
2 teaspoons brown sugar
2 teaspoons Worcestershire sauce
½ teaspoon dried oregano, crushed
½ teaspoon chili powder
½ teaspoon dry mustard
2 bay leaves
2 cloves garlic, minced

● Brush barbecue sauce on the partially baked chicken wings. Bake for 10 minutes, then turn and brush barbecue sauce on the other side. Bake for 5 to 10 minutes more or till chicken is tender. Makes 12 or 24 servings.

Smoky Cheese Log

Pictured on pages 80–81.

For 12

For 24

½ of an 8-ounce package
cream cheese,
cut up (4 ounces)
¾ cup shredded smoked
cheddar cheese
(3 ounces)
¼ cup shredded Swiss
cheese (1 ounce)
2 tablespoons butter *or*
margarine, cut up
1 tablespoon dry white
wine *or* milk
½ teaspoon prepared
horseradish

● Bring cream cheese, cheddar cheese, Swiss cheese, and butter or margarine to room temperature. In a mixer bowl beat cheeses and butter or margarine with an electric mixer till combined. Beat in wine or milk and horseradish. Cover and chill for 2 hours.

1 8-ounce package cream
cheese, cut up
1½ cups shredded smoked
cheddar cheese
(6 ounces)
½ cup shredded Swiss
cheese (2 ounces)
¼ cup butter *or* margarine,
cut up
2 tablespoons dry white
wine *or* milk
1 teaspoon prepared
horseradish

¼ cup finely chopped
pecans *or* walnuts
2 tablespoons snipped
parsley
Assorted crackers

● Combine pecans or walnuts and parsley. On waxed paper shape cheese mixture into a log about 6 inches long (when serving 24, shape into 2 logs). Roll log in nut-parsley mixture, pressing lightly into log. Wrap in clear plastic wrap. Chill about 3 hours or till firm. To serve, unwrap and serve with crackers. Makes 1 or 2 logs.

½ cup finely chopped
pecans *or* walnuts
¼ cup snipped parsley
Assorted crackers

Tomato-Avocado Dip

Pictured on pages 80–81.

For 12		For 24
2 slices bacon	● In a small skillet cook bacon till crisp. Drain well. Crumble bacon and set aside.	**4 slices bacon**
1 large avocado, halved, seeded, and peeled **1 medium tomato, peeled, seeded, and finely chopped** **½ cup dairy sour cream** **¼ cup grated Parmesan cheese** **2 green onions, finely chopped** **1 tablespoon lemon juice** **Dash bottled hot pepper sauce** **1 tablespoon milk (optional)**	● In a medium bowl mash avocado. Stir in tomato, sour cream, Parmesan cheese, green onion, lemon juice, hot pepper sauce, and reserved bacon. Add milk to thin the consistency of the dip, if desired.	**2 large avocados, halved, seeded, and peeled** **2 medium tomatoes, peeled, seeded, and finely chopped** **1 cup dairy sour cream** **½ cup grated Parmesan cheese** **4 green onions, finely chopped** **2 tablespoons lemon juice** **Several dashes bottled hot pepper sauce** **2 tablespoons milk (optional)**
Assorted vegetable dippers	● Transfer mixture to a serving bowl. Cover and chill. Serve with vegetable dippers. Makes 2 or 4 cups.	**Assorted vegetable dippers**

Sangria Sipper

Pictured on pages 80–81.

For 12

2	750-milliliter bottles rosé wine, chilled
¾	cup sugar-and-lemon-flavored iced tea mix
1	orange, thinly sliced
1	lemon, thinly sliced (optional)
2	10-ounce bottles carbonated water, chilled
1	cup sliced fresh strawberries (optional)
	Ice

● In a large pitcher combine rosé wine and iced tea mix. Add orange slices and lemon slices, if desired. Cover and chill. Just before serving, pour carbonated water down the side of the pitcher. Gently stir in sliced fresh strawberries, if desired. Serve over ice. Makes 12 or 24 (8-ounce) servings.

For 24

4	750-milliliter bottles rosé wine, chilled
1½	cups sugar-and-lemon-flavored iced tea mix
2	oranges, thinly sliced
1	lemon, thinly sliced (optional)
4	10-ounce bottles carbonated water, chilled
2	cups sliced fresh strawberries (optional)
	Ice

What Should I Serve?

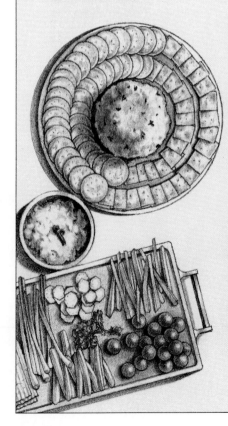

Deciding what foods to serve at a party is always a tough decision—there are so many delicious choices. Here are some tips to keep in mind when planning your menu.

● Serve a combination of hot and cold appetizers. How many of each depends on your refrigerator space and how many appetizers you can keep warm at once.

● Team-up foods with contrasting textures—crisp and crunchy crackers and vegetables work well with creamy dips or spreads.

● Consider flavors and foods that will appeal to your guests. If you don't know what they like, stick to mildly flavored foods. For adventuresome friends, pick out some exotic recipes you've been dying to try.

● Choose appetizers with a variety of flavors. For example, foods all flavored with curry or chili powder will end up tasting the same.

● If you're also serving a meal, match your appetizers to the theme of the meal—Italian antipasto with spaghetti or Chinese egg rolls with moo shu pork.

● Remember that *you* are a part of your party. Avoid dishes that keep you in the kitchen, away from your guests and the fun!

Muchas Margaritas

6 ounces tequila (¾ cup)
4 ounces frozen limeade concentrate (½ cup)
⅓ cup orange liqueur
20 to 24 ice cubes (about 3 cups)

● In a blender container combine tequila, concentrate, and orange liqueur. Cover and blend till smooth. With blender running, add ice cubes, one at a time, through hole in lid, blending till slushy. Pour into prepared glasses (see tip, right). Makes 8 (4-ounce) servings.

● **Very Berry Margaritas:** In a blender container combine the tequila, limeade concentrate, and orange liqueur. Add one 10-ounce package *frozen strawberries,* broken up. Cover and blend until smooth. Add ice as directed for Muchas Margaritas.

● **Gorgeous Grape Margaritas:** In a blender container combine the tequila, one 6-ounce can frozen *grape juice concentrate,* and orange liqueur. Omit limeade concentrate. Cover and blend until smooth. Add ice as directed for Muchas Margaritas.

● **Banana Margaritas:** In a blender container combine the tequila, limeade concentrate, orange liqueur, and 2 cups cut-up ripe *bananas.* Cover and blend until smooth. Add ice as directed for Muchas Margaritas.

● **Apricotta Margaritas:** In a blender container combine the tequila, limeade concentrate, orange liqueur, and one 16-ounce can *unpeeled apricot halves or peach slices,* drained. Cover and blend until smooth. Add ice as directed for Muchas Margaritas.

For lots of folks, a margarita without salt is like a movie without popcorn. Give your margaritas that bartender's flair by rubbing the rim of each glass with a little lime juice or a lime wedge. Invert glasses into a shallow dish of coarse salt, then shake off excess salt.

Frozen Daiquiri Slush

Try a trick similar to the one for margaritas when you're serving daiquiris. Rub the rim of your glasses in water, and dip them into granulated or powdered sugar.

3 cups water
1 6-ounce can frozen lemonade concentrate
1 6-ounce can frozen limeade concentrate
1 juice can rum (¾ cup)
¼ cup sugar

● In a medium mixing bowl stir together water, lemonade concentrate, limeade concentrate, rum, and sugar. Pour into a 9x5x3-inch loaf pan. Cover pan with foil. Freeze overnight.

Lime wedges (optional)

● To serve, scrape the top of the frozen mixture with a spoon to form a slush. Spoon slush into chilled glasses. Garnish with lime wedges, if desired. Makes about 6 (8-ounce) servings.

● **Frozen Fruit Daiquiri Slush:** In a blender container place one 16-ounce package frozen *unsweetened peach slices,* one 10-ounce package frozen *sliced strawberries, or* one 10-ounce package frozen *red raspberries;* add ¾ cup *rum.* Cover and blend till smooth. Transfer to a large mixing bowl. Stir in 3 cups *water,* one 6-ounce can frozen *lemonade concentrate,* and one 6-ounce can frozen *limeade concentrate.* Freeze and serve as directed above. Makes about 8 (8-ounce) servings.

Make-Believe Champagne

1 32-ounce bottle carbonated water, chilled
1 32-ounce bottle ginger ale, chilled
1 24-ounce bottle unsweetened white grape juice, chilled
Party Ice Cubes (see recipe, right)

● In a large pitcher combine carbonated water, ginger ale, and grape juice. Pour over Party Ice Cubes in chilled champagne glasses or wineglasses. Serve immediately. Makes about 20 (4-ounce) servings.

Dress up your party drinks with these easy Party Ice Cubes: Place small pieces of *fruit* (berries or melon balls, for example), small sprigs of *fresh mint, or* ½-inch strips of *orange or lemon peel* into the compartments of ice cube trays. Add enough water to fill, then freeze.

Bar Basics

Relax! Successful bartending doesn't require a degree in mixology. Just keep these tips in mind:
● Don't be tempted to buy out the liquor store. Choose only the liquors you know your guests will drink. If you're unsure, stick with the basics: whiskey, Scotch whisky, gin, vodka, rum, and vermouth for cocktails; wine and beer to drink alone.
● On the average, expect guests to drink 1 to 3 cocktails an hour. If you use 1½ ounces of liquor for each drink, you'll get about 16 drinks from each 750-milliliter bottle (fifth) of liquor. When ordering beer for a party, allow about 12 ounces per guest for every half hour to hour.
● Buy plenty of mixers—carbonated water, tonic water, and ginger ale. Allow about a quart-size bottle for every 3 persons.
● Remember to make a variety of nonalcoholic beverages available for nondrinkers. Carbonated beverages, fruit and vegetable juices, bottled mineral water, coffee, and tea are all popular.
● Don't forget the ice. Allow about a pound of cubes per person, a little more for longer parties (or for parties on hot days).
● You don't need a wide selection of bar glasses. Ten- or 12-ounce all-purpose glasses and 9- or 10-ounce stemmed wineglasses will work for nearly every drink.

Vodka Slush

3½ cups boiling water ½ cup sugar 1 tea bag	● In a large saucepan combine boiling water and sugar, stirring constantly till sugar dissolves. Add tea bag and steep for 3 to 5 minutes. Remove and discard tea bag. Cool.	**Change both the character and color of this cool refresher by stirring in a different flavored vodka and frozen concentrate.**
1 cup cherry-flavored vodka 1 6-ounce can frozen orange juice concentrate	● Stir vodka and orange juice into sugar mixture. Pour into a 9x5x3-inch baking pan. Freeze overnight.	
Carbonated water	● Before serving, use a large spoon to scrape across the surface of the frozen mixture. Spoon into chilled glasses. Pour carbonated water over mixture in glasses and stir gently to make a slush. Makes about 10 (4-ounce) servings.	

Hot Buttered Rum and Cider

7 cups apple cider *or* apple juice ⅓ cup packed brown sugar	● In a large saucepan combine apple cider or apple juice and brown sugar.	**Your crockery cooker is just the thing for serving large quantities of hot beverages. To keep drinks from getting too hot, use the low-heat setting.**
4 inches stick cinnamon 1 teaspoon whole allspice 1 teaspoon whole cloves Peel of 1 lemon, cut into strips	● For spice bag, place cinnamon, allspice, cloves, and lemon peel in a cheesecloth bag and tie. Add spice bag to saucepan with cider mixture.	
1 to 1½ cups rum	● Bring cider mixture to boiling, then reduce heat. Simmer, covered, for 15 minutes. Remove and discard spice bag. Stir in rum.	
Butter *or* margarine	● Before serving, pour into mugs. Float about ½ *teaspoon* butter or margarine on each. Makes about 10 (6-ounce) servings.	
	● **Hot Buttered Cider:** Prepare as directed above, *except* use 8½ cups *apple cider or apple juice,* reduce brown sugar to ¼ cup, and omit rum.	

Spiced Dessert Coffee

8	**cups cold water**
⅔	**cup ground coffee**
4	**inches stick cinnamon**
1	**teaspoon whole cloves**

1	**cup coffee liqueur**

● Put water in a 10-cup electric percolator. Place coffee, cinnamon, and cloves into coffee-maker basket. Prepare according to manufacturer's directions.

● Before serving, remove basket and stir in coffee liqueur. Pour into heat-proof glasses or cups. Makes about 12 (6-ounce) servings.

● **Café Alexander:** Prepare Spiced Dessert Coffee as directed above, *except* substitute 1 tablespoon *crème de cacao* and 1 tablespoon *brandy* for the coffee liqueur per serving.

● **Irish Coffee:** Prepare Spiced Dessert Coffee as directed above, *except* substitute 1 tablespoon *Irish whiskey* and 2 teaspoons *sugar* for the coffee liqueur per serving.

● **Café Nut:** Prepare Spiced Dessert Coffee as directed above, *except* substitute 2 tablespoons *Amaretto or hazelnut liqueur* for the coffee liqueur per serving.

Offer your guests a choice of after-dinner coffees. Just make the Spiced Dessert Coffee without the liqueur, and let your guests tailor their own coffee according to one of the recipe variations at right.

Piña Coladas

1 cup rum
1 6-ounce can frozen
   pineapple juice
   concentrate
½ cup cream of coconut
   Ice cubes

● In a blender container combine rum, pineapple juice concentrate, and cream of coconut. Add enough ice cubes (about 4½ cups) to blender container to measure 5 cups total mixture. Cover and blend till slushy.

Pineapple chunks
   (optional)
Maraschino cherries
   (optional)

● To serve, pour into chilled cocktail glasses. Garnish with pineapple chunks and maraschino cherries, if desired. Makes 5 (8-ounce) servings.

● **Nonalcoholic Piña Coladas:** Prepare as directed above, *except* omit the rum and add ½ cup *water* and 1 teaspoon *vanilla*.

A single sip from this tropical refresher conjures up visions of sun-drenched white-sand beaches, thatch-roofed beach bars, and palm trees.

Perky Perked Punch

3 6-ounce cans
   unsweetened pineapple
   juice (2¼ cups)
2 cups cranberry juice
   cocktail
1 cup water
1 6-ounce can frozen
   lemonade concentrate,
   thawed
⅓ cup packed brown sugar

● In a 10-cup electric percolator combine pineapple juice, cranberry juice cocktail, water, thawed lemonade concentrate, and brown sugar.

6 inches stick cinnamon,
   broken
1 teaspoon whole cloves
1 teaspoon whole allspice

● Place cinnamon, cloves, and allspice into coffee-maker basket. Prepare according to manufacturer's directions. To serve, pour into heat-proof glasses or cups. Makes about 8 (6-ounce) servings.

No electric percolator in your house? No problem. Just combine the fruit juices, water, and brown sugar in a large saucepan. Tie up the spices in a cheesecloth bag and add them to the saucepan. Bring the mixture to a boil, then reduce the heat and simmer about 10 minutes. Remove the spice bag and ladle into glasses or cups.

Cranberry-Wine Cocktail

2 cups rosé wine *or* burgundy, chilled
2 cups cranberry juice cocktail, chilled
1 6-ounce can frozen pineapple juice concentrate

● In a large pitcher combine rosé wine or burgundy, cranberry cocktail, and pineapple concentrate, stirring until concentrate is dissolved.

This full-bodied drink easily converts into a winter warm-up. Heat it on the stove or in the microwave, then serve in mugs.

Frozen pineapple chunks, *or* frosted fresh cranberries (optional)

● Pour into chilled cocktail or wineglasses. Garnish each with frozen pineapple chunks or frosted cranberries on a toothpick, if desired. Makes about 10 (4-ounce) servings.

Creamy Coffee Liqueur Punch

½ cup coffee liqueur
¼ cup milk
2 tablespoons crème de cacao
1 quart vanilla ice cream

● In a blender container combine coffee liqueur, milk, and crème de cacao. Spoon in vanilla ice cream. Cover and blend till smooth.

Beautiful chocolate curls are as easy as a flick of the wrist when you follow our directions.

Chocolate curls (optional) (see tip, right)

● Pour mixture into chilled glasses. Garnish with chocolate curls, if desired. Makes about 6 (4-ounce) servings.

Let a bar of milk chocolate come to room temperature. Carefully draw a vegetable peeler across the chocolate, allowing the chocolate to curl as you pull. (For small curls, use one of the narrow sides of the chocolate; for large curls, use one of the wide surfaces.) Transfer the curls to the drinks by inserting a toothpick through one end and carefully lifting.

Gazpacho Marys

1 12-ounce can (1½ cups)
    vegetable juice cocktail,
    chilled
3 ice cubes

½ of a stalk of celery, cut up
¼ of a medium green
    pepper, seeded and
    cut up
¼ of a medium carrot,
    cut up
2 thin slices onion, cut up
2 ·teaspoons lemon juice
    Few drops bottled hot
    pepper sauce
½ cup vodka
    Cracked ice

● Place vegetable juice cocktail in a blender container. With blender running, add ice cubes, one at a time, through hole in lid, blending until smooth.

● Add celery, green pepper, carrot, onion, lemon juice, and hot pepper sauce to blender. Cover and blend for 30 seconds. Stir in vodka. Strain mixture through a sieve lined with cheesecloth, if desired. Serve over ice. Makes about 5 (4-ounce) servings.

Garnish these jazzed-up Bloody Marys with celery sticks, cucumber spears, or lemon wedges as a garnish.

Tequila Punch

2 cups tequila
½ cup lemon juice
1 46-ounce can
    unsweetened grapefruit
    juice, chilled
1 12-ounce can ginger ale,
    chilled
    Cracked ice

● In a large pitcher combine tequila and lemon juice. Slowly pour in grapefruit juice and ginger ale. Serve over ice. Makes 12 to 15 (6-ounce) servings.

When there's no time to make a punch like this one, turn to two-ingredient Wine Spritzers.
   Fill wineglasses with a ratio of two-thirds *dry white wine* and one-third *carbonated water or ginger ale.* Stir gently to mix. (For 4 servings, you'll need one 750-milliliter bottle *dry white wine* and about 2 cups *carbonated water or ginger ale.*)

Index